GRIEF AND GRATITUDE

Embrace Your Soul's Journey to Joy, Love, and Abundance After Loss

Nancy Jalowiecki Sullivan, M.ED

Grief and Gratitude: Embrace Your Soul's Journey to Joy, Love, and Abundance After Loss
www.griefandgratitudebook.com

Copyright © 2022 Nancy Jalowiecki Sullivan

Paperback ISBN:

All rights reserved. No portion of this book may be reproduced mechanically, electronically, or by any other means, including photocopying, without permission of the publisher or author except in the case of brief quotations embodied in critical articles and reviews. It is illegal to copy this book, post it to a website, or distribute it by any other means without permission from the publisher or author.

References to internet websites (URLs) were accurate at the time of writing. Authors and the publishers are not responsible for URLs that may have expired or changed since the manuscript was prepared.

Limits of Liability and Disclaimer of Warranty
The author and publisher shall not be liable for your misuse of the enclosed material. This book is strictly for informational and educational purposes only.

Warning – Disclaimer
The purpose of this book is to educate and entertain. The author and/or publisher do not guarantee that anyone following these techniques, suggestions, tips, ideas, or strategies will become successful. The author and/or publisher shall have neither liability nor responsibility to anyone with respect to any loss or damage caused, or alleged to be caused, directly or indirectly by the information contained in this book.

Medical Disclaimer
The medical or health information in this book is provided as an information resource only, and is not to be used or relied on for any diagnostic or treatment purposes. This information is not intended to be patient education, does not create any patient-physician relationship, and should not be used as a substitute for professional diagnosis and treatment.

No content on this book should ever be used as a substitute for direct medical advice from your doctor or other qualified clinician. This book does not intend to diagnose or treat any physical or mental illness. Rather, it shares the author's own experiences in healing after the loss of a still born baby and shortly after, her husband.

Publisher
10-10-10 Publishing
Canada

Printed in Canada and the United States of America

Table of Contents

Dedication.. vii
Foreword ix
A Note from the Author xi

Chapter 1 - Heal Your Soul 1
Chapter 2 - My Stages of Understanding 27
Chapter 3 - Walking into the Unknown 51
Chapter 4 - Life Is Everything 71
Chapter 5 - Healing & Growth 93
Chapter 6 - Happy Again 119
Chapter 7 - Children & Grieving 143
Chapter 8 - Make the Shift From Pain to Power 163
Chapter 9 - Thoughts Become Things 185
Chapter 10 - You Are Worthy! 215

Acknowledgements 241
About the Author 259
Connect with the Author 261

Dedication

This book is dedicated to my late husband, Edward Matthew Jalowiecki, and Mike's late wife, Maria Bridget Sullivan.

We loved you yesterday, we love you today, and you will forever be in our hearts. There is no US without YOU. Thank you for trusting us to raise our daughters with love, courage and dignity, and for helping us to realize that we are worthy of a fulfilled and happy life, of which you will always be a part.

To Mama Mercedes from whom I learned so much and who loved me unconditionally. You will forever be close to my heart.

To Uncle Joe whose memory will always be with us. Thank you for all the love you gave us and for treating Kaya and Navah as your granddaughters.

To Mr. Cruz, my colleague and my friend. I will always love you and appreciate your help, guidance and conversations shared from the heart. You showed me so much love after Ed's passing; and little did I know that shortly after, we were going to lose you. Your legacy will forever live in the hearts of every soul you touched, mine included.

For bonus material go to www.griefandgratitudebook.com

To the souls that had to depart with their hearts filled with love and bravery, as saying goodbye to loved ones is never easy.

To every innocent and resilient child who has lost a parent prematurely and, as a young warrior, had to endure the loss and move through life with faith and determination.

To you reading this book, for your unconditional love, support, and courage. This world is a better place because of you.

To Panchito, my chihuahua, thank you for over 15 years of love and companionship.

Foreword

Have you recently lost a loved one, and are now feeling like grief has taken over your life, leaving little room for joy, love and fulfillment? Do you want to regain some of your old self? Do you want to dream again? Are you ready to step out of the darkness and allow the light back in?

I hope you were able to answer *yes* to the last two questions. If you are grieving, but you know that there has to be more for you in this life, would you be willing to do the work to feel better? Would you like to have more tools to help you journey through your grief, to a life that makes you excited to get up in the morning again?

If you answered *yes* to these questions as well, then you have picked up the perfect book. *Grief and Gratitude* takes you on a journey from love and loss, to adventure and new-found happiness. Nancy Jalowiecki Sullivan is no stranger to grief. Just after losing her son, she lost her husband after a short battle with cancer. Left with two young girls in a situation she had never imagined she would be in, Nancy knew that she could either let herself slip into the darkness, or she could embark on the journey of a lifetime.

Nancy chose life, and her story will inspire you to choose life too. The journey she shares with you is one of pain, old and new

For bonus material go to www.griefandgratitudebook.com

love, adventure, growth, friendships, and spirituality. It is with loving arms that she welcomes you in, and bravely shares with you how she came to accept that the grief she was experiencing was meant to be part of her life experience. You will walk with her as she embarks on a great adventure that leads her into a new chapter in her life. A chapter filled with healing, love and hope.

Ultimately, Nancy realized after her husband passed that she was worthy of happiness again. She shares with you her personal experiences in a way that is engaging and easy to read. You will find yourself drawn into her story in a way that makes you want to keep turning to the next page. Not only that, Nancy invites you to embark on your own journey of self-discovery by giving you useful tools to help you move forward in your own healing.

Grief and Gratitude was written for you, and you will not regret picking it up. YOU are worthy. YOUR life is important. NOW is the time to awaken your inner joy and step into a life that you love. Get ready to begin the next chapter of your life; one that is filled with absolute abundance!

Loral Langemeier
The Millionaire Maker

A Note from the Author

Dear Reader,

Greetings to you. It's with joy and excitement that I welcome you to my book. My hope is that you use it as inspiration in your own healing journey.

I was inspired to write this book after the loss of my husband, Ed, of 10 years which made me a young widow. This shift caused me to reassess and figure out what I wanted in my life after embarking on a new journey, one that wasn't planned.

Finding myself overwhelmed by Ed's death, and with two young daughters and a dog that depended on me, I had to make a decision: Do I want to live in sorrow, suffering and in the past? Or do I surrender and trust that my grief is a part of my journey, for my highest good and the evolution of my soul?

The choice was clear. I knew that surrendering and consciously focusing on the present moment was all I had. I also needed to refocus my lens to see my life just the way it was and accept it without blaming others or myself or feeling like a victim.

Shortly after Ed's death, I began sharing my story. I noticed that the more I shared, the more I learned about those who I had shared with and listened to. Not only were we learning about each

For bonus material go to ...

other on a deeper level, but we were also creating a safe space to connect from the heart and heal.

At the end of sharing my story, I would hear, "Thank you so much for sharing your story. It has really impacted me," "I am getting goosebumps listening to your story," or "You have empowered me to focus on my goals and desires."

It was after these encounters, with known and unknown souls, that I realized that many of you, and I, shared the pain, guilt, uncertainty, loneliness, that came from traumatic experiences of the past. You became my motivation to write this book, to continue sharing my story and to provide you with the opportunity to focus on your own healing and liberate yourself from suffering.

There were strategies that helped me work through my grief and, as a result, find happiness and love again. I gave myself the opportunity to embrace my life as it was unfolding before my eyes. The strategies I used and the actions that I took are shared with you in this book. My intention is that they will serve as a vehicle to help you accept, heal and transform your life. You're alive. You have a purpose. You are worthy of living a fulfilled and happy life.

The exercises provided in this book at the end of each chapter are meant to empower and provide you with the space and opportunity you need to release the pain from your heart. Writing is very powerful. This is your time to connect and allow yourself to go back to a painful situation, see it as it was, accept it and then release it in your own time. You decide to eliminate or embrace each experience based on how it makes you feel. These techniques are steppingstones to help you discover your golden self, the

www.griefandgratitudebook.com

person that you really are! They will also provide you with the knowledge and understanding that many of the answers to your own questions can be found deep inside you, and that you are a powerful being that can transform your life. Complete as many or as few of these exercises based on what resonates with you. These are optional and are always available to come back to at a later time.

Grief and Gratitude is a life story written from the heart and shared with love to uplift your spirit, bring hope and inspire you to step into your life. No matter where you've been or come from, whatever your skin color is or your gender, you are special and unique, and worthy of a happy, abundant, and fulfilled life. Don't be afraid to take your flight and make the decision on how high you want to fly. You are in control and have all you need to embark your journey. Enjoy the adventure!

Thank you for allowing me to share my story with you.

**With love and gratitude,
Nancy Jalowiecki Sullivan**

Chapter 1

Heal Your Soul

"And so I wait. I wait for time to heal the pain and raise me to my feet once again, so that I can start a new path, my own path, the one that will make me whole again."
– Jack Canfield

1

Grief is a process. Yours will be different from mine. Mine will be different from that of my children. Theirs will be different from that of their friends. But with all of that said, it is a process you need to undertake. Go through it and allow it to change you. Allow yourself to cry, to scream, to be angry, to retreat from the world and to feel everything you need to feel to come out on the other side, stronger. You matter. Your life matters. Grief does not define you. Death does not define you. Life and connecting with your soul does.

How you choose to live your life going forward is up to you. Only you can make the choice to live again. Only you can seek the help you need to rise up from the ashes and embrace the real you. Only you can find happiness for yourself!

I am here to tell you that happiness is possible. I don't know what stage and type of grief you are in at this moment. You may still be struggling in a dark place, feeling as though this world can't do anything but knock you down, again and again and again. It's okay. I've been in some very dark places of my own and I'm here to tell you, there is light, and you will find it again.

You must know this is true or you wouldn't be here with me, reading this book. Deep down, you know this can't be it. You know life has more for you. You have the opportunity to heal and

For bonus material go to ...

connect with your soul. I want to begin this book by sharing with you a chapter in my own story:

My husband was only 42 years old on the day he died.

I had just received a message from his best friend.

"Jay, is Ed awake?" asked Scott.

"Yes," I started to write, when I felt the urge to look up and make sure that Ed was indeed awake, and then right before my eyes, I captured this glowing, shimmering light moving downward, taking Ed's life essence with it. Immediately, I knew his soul was leaving his body and that his journey in this life was over.

The part of the body left behind by this tangible glowing light that was moving downward, had dull skin and was lifeless.

In shock and shaking, I got up and screamed, "Amore, I told you not to leave me and you're leaving me!"

I held him and cried, for a while knowing that no matter what I said or did, he had to go. He didn't have a choice. It was his time. He was so young, and it happened so quickly.

I went back to just a few months and remembered that during our second family trip to the Dominican Republic in August of 2018, Ed decided that this would be where we would retire. He loved the weather, surfing in Playa Encanto and practicing his Spanish with the locals.

Shortly after returning to New York City, we started looking at properties for sale in Puerto Plata. Nothing materialized and, in a matter of a few weeks, Ed was given a diagnosis that changed our lives' course forever.

Ed went from being the healthiest patient in our community clinic to just having 1 to 3 months to live without treatment. Initially, because of his excellent health, he had a good prognosis. Little did we know at that time that the survival rate of patients diagnosed with myeloid leukemia is about 20%. We followed up with all recommended treatments, but nothing worked. We kept facing one challenge after the other.

Ed was getting tired and weaker, and I was getting desperate and said, "Ed, visualize that you are healthy and that you and I are celebrating our 10-year anniversary!"

He responded and said, "Amore, it's not my mind; it's my body giving up on me!"

I cried. We held hands quietly for a long time.

I would come home from the hospital and our girls kept asking, "When is Daddy coming home?"

Every time, I answered with the only response I could think of: "Daddy will come home soon."

Ed had a small family. He was the only child and was raised by this mother, Sharon, and his father, Edward Paul. His parents divorced when he was a teenager. I never met Ed's father because he had passed before we met. Every month, we would go to Connecticut for 2 or 3 days to visit and spend time with Sharon. However, this time she was visiting us since Ed was hospitalized. She was very worried.

Another memory of mine was when we were visiting Ed at the hospital. My younger daughter, Navah, who was five years old, asked, "Daddy, if Mommy gets leukemia like you, who will take care of us? Grandma?" She pointed at her paternal grandma, who was sitting in a large chair leaning on her walker. Ed and I just looked at each other. We could not believe Navah's question. It hit us both.

Ed calmly responded by saying, "Sweetheart, it is very unlikely that Mommy will get leukemia, but if anything were to happen to Mommy, we have chosen the perfect family for you and Kaya to stay with."

Tears went down my cheeks as he spoke. And I knew how hard this was for him ... It was an intense and deep conversation that I was not ready to have at that time.

This life is good but it's not fair at times. But it is what it is, I thought to myself.

I just knew that I had to find the courage and the strength to be there physically and emotionally for Ed, Sharon, and for both of my daughters. I needed to hold my family together with unwavering faith and determination.

I did my best. As Ed was dying, there were moments when I felt like I might break, but I held it together. There was so much to be done, and I needed to be brave and bold.

Even though I knew his death was inevitable, at first, I did not fully accepted it. I thought we had more time. Once he was gone and the reality of it all set in, I felt as though everything was scary. My world had gone completely dark. I felt so sad for Ed, and I remember when he said to me in one of my visits to the hospital, "Amore, I am not ready to leave my daughters ... they are so young ... I don't want to leave you alone." I was suddenly drowning in a river of tears and uncertainty.

The Universe Provides

When you are drowning in your own river of uncertainty, when you can't seem to pull yourself up to breathe, when you are grieving the loss of a life partner, a child, a parent, a good friend, or a loved one, things in the world don't feel right. Sometimes, depending on the situation, everything is different. Your life feels upside down and your new normal feels heavy, painful, and impossible to navigate. It may feel as though the raging river will keep dragging you without giving you any clear indication as to where you are headed or even why you are headed there.

You don't understand why you've lost the person you love so much. I am not here to tell you with absolute certainty that things happen for a reason, but what I can share is my own experiences as I walk my own life path. I see my life experiences like attending school, mastering the content that I was meant to learn, and

For bonus material go to ...

graduating. As I move through the courses in my life, learn, and graduate, I can then reflect and put into practice what I've learned. I know for sure that each experience has contributed to who I've become, and that I have learned from each one, even the incredibly difficult ones.

Ed and I lost our first baby at 36 weeks. I cannot explain with words how devastated we were, but I will try. It was like an invisible force was crushing my entire body. Or like I had been hit by a truck and managed to get back up somehow, even though I didn't want to. And it seemed to hit Ed worse than me.

Our first baby boy, whom we named Kai Alexander, at 20 weeks, was so close to coming into this world to join us and we already loved him so much. We were ready to welcome him into our lives as we had in our hearts. We never imagined that he would be stillborn. When you get that close to seeing your pregnancy to full term, you just can't imagine not returning home with your baby. I want people to know that not every couple has a happy ending. Not every couple returns home with the baby they were waiting for.

Instead of making the final preparations in our home for the new arrival, we were planning his funeral. Because Ed was struggling, I knew I had to step up and carry the torch. It never crossed my mind that I would be doing the same for Ed only a few short years later.

In many ways, although it was a different kind of loss, the death of our first baby prepared me for the loss of my husband. One of the simplest ways was in planning for the funeral during a time of loneliness despite all the people around and when my brain was filled with negative thoughts; I at least could do this without confusion.

On a deeper level, it prepared me for my journey with grief for a second time. Did it make it easier? No. Are there times when I still feel pain for the loss of my son and my husband? Yes. But even though I have my moments of sadness, I am at peace and no longer suffering. It was a process, and it took me some time to get here, and I continue to accept, hope, and heal.

To end my suffering, I had to go within, and through the process of grieving and accepting that my path has peaks and valleys. Each valley prepared me for the peaks and provided me with a clearer perspective in my life. I had to live in it. This was something that no one could do for me. I had to do it on my own. Many of us experience a desire to try to ignore; to go back to some kind of normal without really dealing with the stages of complicated emotions grief will force you to go through. This is normal. It's painful. At times, it's unbearable. You want to run from it. I am here to tell you that if you run from it, you are denying yourself a great gift. When you allow yourself to find the lesson in the pain, you allow yourself to feel, connect with your emotions, and develop an understanding that you are not alone. This is when you step into who you really are and walk into your greater purpose in life.

For bonus material go to ...

My Greater Purpose

"Strength doesn't come from what you can do. It comes from overcoming the things you once thought you couldn't."
– Rikki Rogers

For those of you meeting me for the first time, I would like to share a few words so that you can get to know the author behind this real-life story you're holding in your hands.

The thought of becoming a widow had never crossed my mind. Ever! But there I was after almost ten years of a happy and peaceful marriage, with two young girls and a dog, making arrangements for my husband's funeral. My baby boy, Kai Alexander, had taught me exactly what I needed to do, which allowed me to get through the process with greater ease.

I truly believe that each challenging experience I've been through in my life has contributed to who I've become and has fulfilled my life's journey in this lifetime and the healing of my soul.

It's no coincidence that I had to go through each and every experience to be exactly where I am today. Duality has allowed me to appreciate, value, and develop a deeper connection with my life and all living things, accepting and respecting that no matter what, life is beautiful and filled with magic. Based on my life experiences, I have come to the realization that my path was decided even before I got here. For me, this was quite intense. The more I accept myself, and others, I can't stop noticing all the beauty that surrounds me as I mindfully walk my own life path.

I know that every adversity has brought me strength, knowledge, and transformation. Certainly, losing Ed was a big one for me.

In this book, I will share with you my journey through the loss of a baby and my husband at a young age, to be where I am today: I am a woman who has stepped into her purpose with courage, strength, and an unwavering desire to use my experience to help others. My mission in life, as I understand it now, is to help others to become their best selves by learning from their challenges and recognizing their own personal value to the world around them.

The biggest lesson I have learned is that when you don't understand what is happening in your life, you must simply let go and trust the journey. Your life has meaning. You have a purpose. You picked up this book because even if it is hard to see in this moment, you know it. Deep down, you want to heal; you want to walk forward on your own life journey.

I hope that sharing my story and how I was able to find my own life purpose again, will support you as you continue on your healing path. Throughout the book, I will provide exercises and affirmations to inspire you to reflect on yourself, your feelings, your life, and your desires. I will also leave some space for you to reflect directly in the pages of this book, but I recommend that you either have an accompanying journal for times when you need more space to go deeper, or an ongoing document on your

For bonus material go to ...

computer. Do what works best for you, but I believe that you will get the most from the stories and lessons I share by tying them back to your own life and experiences. It's your story! We all have one ... it has brought us to this moment. The beauty of it all is that your past does not determine your future; you do.

Many widows often go through a stage where they feel that their life is over. I know. I've been there. I am on the other side of it and am here to tell you that it is not! Whether you believe it or not, you can find love again. You and your children (if you have them) will be happy again, and you can pursue new dreams, like going back to school or traveling to parts of the world you've always wanted to see.

Let's begin!

Reflection Exercise

Have you ever had an experience that transformed your life? You can write about anything here. It can be about your loss, but it could also be about something wonderful. The goal in the exercise is to recognize that you have the ability to be transformed by the world around you. Open yourself back up. Let go!

_____
_____
_____
_____
_____
_____

My Soul's Journey

Before Ed passed, I don't really remember how intuitive I was. Did I allow myself to feel things? Was I open to receiving all of the information the Universe has to share with me? In some ways, probably, but it wasn't until I saw that shimmery glowing energy leaving Ed's body, and the difference it made in his physical presence on this Earth, that I truly woke up to the mystical. Everything is energy!

Now I actively listen. I allow for guidance. I open myself up to receiving by working on my blocks, the obstacles in life I need to overcome. I seek knowledge and understanding, and sometimes these things come from places I'm not always aware of or are able to see. I question myself when I feel closed.

I want to share another story to help you to understand where this is coming from and how the idea of mysticism ties into the lessons that I have learned and am now sharing with you.

One day a good friend of mine wanted to have her cards read. She asked if I wanted to go. When we got there, I let her go in first. I had only really gone because she asked me to. I didn't really have a feeling about it one way or another.

I walked into the room and sat down in front of the psychic.

She smiled and shuffled her cards.

"What would you like to know?"

For bonus material go to ...

I hadn't thought about anything ahead of time, so I asked her to share with me whatever came up. With cards I had pulled laid out in front of her on the table, she started slowly:

"You will have an abundance of love in your life. You will have 3 children... Something happens to the first but the other two will be okay. Shortly after the birth of your third child, your husband will die."

Honestly, I don't remember what she said after that. I walked out of the room feeling a bit stunned.

When my reading concluded, I met with my friend. She was crying but did not really share her message. I told her, with a feeling of disbelief, about the message I received. Disappointed with the experience, we decided to eat some Mexican food and had a margarita to cheer ourselves up. It worked!

The next day, I went into work and met with another friend, Evie, who is kind and intuitive. I felt like sharing with her what the psychic reader saw in my cards the day before.

"Oh wow. Why would she tell you that in this manner? It was insensitive... What are you going to do?"

"I am not sure... I guess that I will prepare for the event, but I'm not sure how. I don't have a husband yet!"

After that day, I forgot all about the revelation from the tarot cards. It didn't even occur to me when I met Ed that an early death was his fate. It wasn't until after he died that Evie called me to check up on how Ed was doing. I started crying and telling her of Ed's passing. I told her I was angry and upset and that I did not see it coming. I also told her that Ed had two bone marrow donors waiting on him, and usually people die waiting for donors. How unfair. She listened and waited, and then in a loving, kind, and gentle voice said, "I am so sorry that you are going through this ... I got very worried back in November when you shared Ed's diagnosis. Do you remember the card reading you had over 15 years ago?" I stopped crying and immediately was transported to that overwhelming moment and could hear the psychic's voice saying, "Shortly after the birth of your third child, your husband will die." I took a few breaths and felt as if Evie had handed me the last piece to complete the puzzle.

The feeling of sadness, of shock, of disbelief ... somehow it all came together. It occurred to me at that moment that I had forgotten because I wasn't supposed to know. I was supposed to lose my first son and my husband. These were experiences that my soul, or the Divine, God, the Universe, wanted me to go through innocently to help me grow, and to help me find my purpose and learn from the experience.

I am so grateful for Ed. Together we shared so much love, and this love created our beautiful family. His death was a part of his journey and linked to mine. Today, I believe he leads me with love. I feel his energy often and know that his light, the one I saw leave his body, is shining on me and our girls.

For bonus material go to ...

Let Your Angels Guide You

Looking back on the moment I witnessed Ed's soul leave his body, I know now that I am more awake. By this, I mean that I am open to receiving knowledge that I may once not have been able to see or understand. My awareness continues to become more expansive each day. As I began writing the opening few paragraphs of this book, I realized that I was ready to experience and actually see Ed's soul leave the body as it was returning to the nonphysical state.

With each new day, I feel that my own ability to see, feel, and hear the message I am given, grows. I am becoming more aware of my own telepathic skills. This is why I share these thoughts with you. Our brains are a bit like a puzzle with a whole bunch of pieces. Some of the pieces are easy to fit together. Some pieces are hidden from us until we are ready to have them—like me forgetting what the psychic had told me. The Universe wasn't ready for me to have that information, so those puzzle pieces hid themselves deep in my brain, not to be recalled until they had a place to fit into the tapestry of my life story.

After I lost Ed, I had no idea where my journey would take me, but I felt like I needed some time with myself. I didn't want to be the victim. I wanted to take control of my life. I wanted to be excited to be alive again. I did something I never thought I could do. I packed a bag, left everything behind, and took a solo trip to the other side of the world. I fought my fear of the unknown. I faced my worry over leaving the girls; Ed and I had never been separated from them. I listened to my heart. I will share more about my journey and how it helped heal my spirit, in future chapters. For now, what I want to share with you is that I believe it taught me to value my own self-worth again. I believe it brought me back to life. I also know that through it all, my angel and my higher self (that part of me that knows everything) were guiding me and helping unfold those experiences I needed to go through and overcome. These experiences were part of my soul's journey.

There are angels all around us guiding us each and every day. There are angels guiding you. Ed, one of my many angels, guided me to meet my soul mate. Yes, you read that right. He helped me find love again. If you would've told me this was possible prior to it actually happening, I would've laughed. But it happened.

Ed's social worker, Alison, who really didn't have to continue working with me after he was gone, was so kind, gentle, and compassionate. She looked up resources and informed me of a program through CancerCare, called Healing Hearts Family Bereavement Camp. This is a weekend retreat that's free of charge for those who are accepted. It brings families together who have lost a loved one to cancer. Alison informed me that this program is very popular and fills up quickly, and that there was an application process and an interview. Acceptance was not guaranteed, but it was worth a try. I listened to her and thanked her. However, I was so overwhelmed with Ed's loss and crying every day that a part of me did not want to apply or go anywhere. However, Alison kept reaching out, wanting to know if I had applied. So, I decided to apply and go and celebrate Ed. I remember having the interview with Claire from CancerCare, and a few days later, I received an email and a call that we were in. We received a list of instructions as to what to prepare to bring with us.

For bonus material go to ...

We started gathering information and selecting photos, and there were so many beautiful memories. The girls and I would cry and hug each other. I wrote a biography about my beloved Ed, who was special and unique. I remember that it took me a few days to write it. Every time I sat in front of my computer to write, I cried and thought about Ed. He had a big heart. He was loving and sensitive, funny, and compassionate. He truly loved these girls, as could be seen by how overprotective he was at times.

I was thinking about how he would always say, "Till death do us part," which was his answer to people who asked us, "Are you together?" I recalled how he would take me out on a date once a month, and we had so much fun. I remember one evening date. We went to three different restaurants, and we were like two high school kids having fun. I smiled, blinked and I was finished writing the biography. It was done, and I felt so good about it. Going through the list and process in preparation for the Healing Hearts Retreat was healing.

Finally, the day came, and we left New York City a bit early to make sure we got to the Poconos in Pennsylvania on time. On our way there, we got stuck in traffic for 8 long hours, and we arrived after midnight. When we got there, I was informed that we and the Sullivan family were the last two families they were waiting for, and that now all members were at the campground.

Mike Sullivan and his daughter, Molly, were the others who arrived after midnight as well. They had been stuck in traffic for 9 hours. Mike almost turned around and went back home, but he decided to continue to the Healing Hearts Retreat for the benefit of his daughter.

But unlike me, Mike had no idea the retreat existed until the last minute. Mike kept bumping into his late wife Maria's wig, and one day he decided that he wanted to donate it. Perhaps someone else in need could use it. Maria never liked it and hardly wore it. He went online to research for the best place and found an organization called CancerCare. He got there with the wig and informed one of CancerCare counselors, Ariana, about his intentions.

They started talking and Mike shared his story about Maria's passing from cancer. Losing Maria was devastating for Mike and both of their daughters, Molly and Keeva. Ariana listened and, shortly after, informed him about the Healing Hearts Bereavement Camp. Coincidentally, a family had just canceled. The retreat had been booked for months. There was now a spot available if he wanted to take it. Mike thought this was a great idea and confirmed that he would attend. He just needed to find care for Keeva because she was too young. Mike reached out to his parents, Papa Mike and Nanny (Maureen), and they were happy to take care of Keeva the weekend of the retreat.

On the first morning, as Kaya, Navah, and I were walking towards the breakfast venue, Mike and Molly were coming out. We greeted each other, not knowing that we were the last two families that had arrived after midnight.

After breakfast, all the kids gathered together out in the field, and the counselors were talking, playing, and getting to know the little ones. The day was sunny, warm, and beautiful. There was a sense of peace and tranquility, wrapped around sadness but welcoming a new day filled with hope. At this time, the adults had

For bonus material go to ...

the opportunity to complete their registration and bring the photos and collected items to display on a memorial table, to celebrate their deceased loved ones.

I went to the room and grabbed the bag that had the things we wanted to display. I walked down to the field and called the girls so that they could join me in setting up Ed's tribute. This was one of the first activities at the retreat, and I thought it was an important thing for us to do as a family. However, my girls ran over and explained that they were playing with a little girl named Molly, who had lost her mommy, Maria, and they did not want to leave her alone.

Navah said, "Mommy, she lost her mommy just like we lost Daddy, and she misses her mommy."

I then decided to leave them at the field playing with Molly. Then, Molly's daddy, Mike, came to the field. We introduced ourselves to each other.

I said to Mike, "Molly just shared with my daughters, Kaya and Navah that she lost her mommy and misses her."

Tears came to Mike's eyes, and he said, "This means the world to me because I've been so worried. Molly has not talked about her mom with anyone since her passing, and I am glad that she is talking about it with your daughters."

I asked Mike if he could watch over the girls playing while I went and set up for Ed. He agreed.

Throughout the retreat, there seemed to always be a reason for us to end up in the same place. Kaya, Navah, and Molly were inseparable. Mike and I ended up in the same support group. When Mike shared Maria's story, the counselor got up and gave me the box of tissues. I could not stop crying. I felt so sad for Maria, and I could only imagine how she was feeling before her passing, having to leave her husband and her two young daughters. I then started to pray and thank God for everything I have and for still being here and able to care for my daughters.

Mike and I also ended up in the same horseback riding activity, and Mike invited us to drive together to the place. I accepted. The first thing Kaya said was, "Mommy, Mr. Mike looks like Daddy but with hair." I did not respond to the comment.

Maria and Ed had found a way to bring us together to find happiness again. Mike and I and our four girls walk forward in life hand in hand. We honor our angels by embracing the happy moments we have with them and using those moments to uplift our souls. I know Ed wouldn't have wanted me to be living in sadness and grief for the remainder of my life. At times, I can almost remember him whispering in my ear, "Go be happy. Take care of you."

For bonus material go to ...

Take Care of You

***"You're going to make it;
You're going to be at peace;
You're going to create, and love, and laugh, and live;
You're going to do great things."***
– Germany Kent

Read that quote again! I promise you are going to make it! I don't know your story. I don't know what you've been through. Even though you are grieving, the only thing I know is that your grief is intensely personal. I also know that you have the strength to find joy in life again, but you can't do it unless you learn to take care of yourself and go within.

The work you do in this book is going to ask you to make yourself and your life the top priority. It is going to ask you to stay present in this moment. Of course, you can still honor the ones you have loved and lost, but you don't have to live in the past to do that.

In a way, this book will also be a kind of self-led workshop. It will question you. It will ask you to step outside your comfort zone. But most importantly, it will ask you to dream big again. It will ask you to recognize just how valuable you are and how much your life matters—for you!

www.griefandgratitudebook.com

Reflection Exercise

What am I most afraid of in this moment?

_____
_____
_____
_____
_____

What is one thing I can do right now to fight that fear?

_____
_____
_____
_____
_____

Affirmation

    At the end of every chapter, I will share with you a positive affirmation and leave a page for you to write it out and reflect on it. If you've never worked with affirmations in the past, there are a few ways you can. Some people find it beneficial to write the affirmation repeatedly while internally reflecting on how they feel about what blocks are coming up for them as they write it out. Some people write it on a piece of paper and put it up on their bathroom mirror so that they can see it every day. Others read the

For bonus material go to ...

affirmation and then write about their blocks and how they plan to overcome them to embrace the affirmation in their daily lives.

Do what works best for you. You can also create your own affirmations.

Your first affirmation is:

I am important. My life has value and I welcome joy into my life!

_____
_____
_____
_____
_____

www.griefandgratitudebook.com

My Notes

For bonus material go to www.griefandgratitudebook.com

My Notes

Chapter 2

My Stages of Understanding

"When you lose someone you can't imagine living without, your heart breaks wide open, and the bad news is you never completely get over the loss. You will never forget them. However, in a backwards way, this is also the good news. They will live on in the warmth of your broken heart that doesn't fully heal back up, and you will continue to grow and experience life, even with your wound. It's like badly breaking an ankle that never heals perfectly, and that still hurts when you dance, but you dance anyway with a slight limp, and this limp just adds to the depth of your performance and the authenticity of your character. The people you lose remain a part of you. Remember them and always cherish the good moments spent with them."
– Christopher Walken

2

As I sit to write this chapter, I am also planning a return trip to the Healing Hearts Retreat. It has been over three years since I lost Ed. In these three years, I have learned to dance again. Some days have been harder than others—some days are still harder than others—but I keep dancing; I keep remembering. This last part is important to me. Yes, I keep moving through life for myself because I am worthy, for my children because they are worthy, and for Ed, who has been the inspiration to write this book.

In this chapter, I want to share more in depth what it was like spending those last months in the hospital with Ed, and the stages of grief I experienced as he was dying, and following his death. No two experiences with death and grief will be the same; however, there are some common stages people often go through in grief: denial, anger, bargaining, depression, and acceptance.

The thing to remember is that you can fluctuate between stages. Just following Ed's death, I would jump from denial to anger to depression all in one day. Before Ed died, I did my best to stay positive. I had so much hope that something would work, that he would get better. Looking back now, I also know that I was experiencing so many emotions simultaneously. Our lives were turned upside down in an instant, never to return to the way they

For bonus material go to ...

were before. I now realize that my grieving started upon his diagnosis.

Shock

When Ed was first diagnosed with acute myeloid leukemia (AML), we both felt shocked. Nothing could have prepared us for that news. AML affects the blood and bone marrow. The conditions are generally called "acute" because the development of the illness is quick and aggressive.

When we walked into Ed's oncologist to confirm the diagnosis, he looked at Ed with sympathy and said the normal greetings.

"I have a room ready for you, Ed."

I could feel Ed panicking beside me. I squeezed his hand just a little tighter.

"What about if I don't want to start the treatment right away that you are recommending?"

Without hesitation, his doctor responded, "Then you will have one to three months to live."

We both stood there staring. Only one to three months. We thought we had decades. We had just been talking about retirement in the Dominican Republic. This could not be happening. How do you lose a whole future in just one sentence?

His doctor felt our energy and quickly added, "But with treatment, you will live longer and perhaps go into complete remission."

"Remission?" I asked.

"Remission is when tests, physical exams, and scans show no sign of the disease."

With tears in my eyes, I turned to Ed, "Amore, you are staying."

"I have no choice," he responded.

Stress

Having Ed in the hospital was a life-changing event that was both draining and stressful for us both. No longer was my life stable and predictable. I not only had to work full time, but I was now 100% responsible for the care of the girls and our dog, Panchito. On top of that, I did all of the grocery shopping, household chores, helped the girls with homework, and went with them to their school events. Life had to move forward. It was important for the girls to have as much stability as we could give them.

Ed's first few weeks at Columbia Presbyterian hospital were hopeful. Everyone was professional, caring, and accommodating. In a short time, the bone marrow transplant unit team provided us with a lot of information, including diet restrictions and treatment plan schedules. The amount of information presented to us was much more overwhelming than we had anticipated. Yet, we continued to lift our spirits and remain hopeful, and soon his unit became our second home.

To protect Ed from exposure to germs, our daughters, Kaya and Navah, could only see their daddy once or twice per week for an hour. These visits needed to be arranged ahead of time with Ed's social worker, Alison, who was so gentle, kind, helpful, and always available.

Ed could not hug his daughters. He would get nervous and give me a worried look when they got too close to him. I had to remind the girls that distance from their dad needed to be kept. He felt terrible that he was unable to hug or kiss them. Sometimes, when the girls needed a hug, he would compromise by just touching their backs. He would say to them all the time: "I can't wait to heal, come home, and give you long hugs."

I remember celebrating Ed's 42nd birthday at the hospital with the girls, not knowing it would be the last birthday we were going to celebrate together.

Trying to Balance a New Unbalanced Life

The fact that I had to work full time, visit Ed at the hospital, and take care of our girls was a load that kept getting heavier and heavier. It was becoming increasingly clear that I was going to break, and then I wouldn't be any good for anyone. I completed the paperwork to take a family leave and learned that it was unpaid for teachers, due to a new UFT contract, but I did it anyway. I had to.

I wanted to be able to spend more time at the hospital to provide Ed with the emotional support I knew he needed. I also felt like Kaya, Navah, and Panchito needed me even more now. I did not want work to get in the way.

Ed expressed concerns about how taking an unpaid family leave was going to affect our family financially, now that he was not working as well. Honestly, that was the last thing on my mind at the moment, but as I was getting ready to submit the application, the doctors advised me to wait to take the family leave until after Ed's bone marrow transplant, since this was the most critical time. Ed was going to need me the most when he was sent back home. The plan was explained: Ed's transplant was scheduled for February 26, 2019. He was going to stay at the hospital until March 30th and then come home around April 1st. I was planning to start my family leave at that time. However, things didn't go as planned.

Go with the Flow

When someone you love is fighting for their life, "Go with the flow" is probably the last thing in the world you want to hear. If you have gone through it, you know how it feels, but you also know it is probably the only thing you can do to remain sane. Sometimes you can plan for the unexpected, but more often than not, you

For bonus material go to …

can't. Let go. I had to learn the hard way that it is easier to stop trying to control a situation that is not yours to control. I had to go through the experience.

The entire time Ed was in the hospital, I felt as if I was drowning in a river of uncertainty. Ed continued developing fevers and was in need of more and more blood transfusions to stay alive. His transplant was postponed due to recurring fevers that would not cease.

I do not think there was a moment during those five months when I was not worried about my husband. I prayed constantly and looked forward to caring for him at home. We were looking forward to Daddy coming home to celebrate Navah's 6th birthday on April 30th. Each day, I could not wait to get out of work to go to the hospital. Then, I would leave the hospital, take the train, and go pick up my daughters from the after-school program.

One day, I went to the hospital and Ed said, "Amore, I would like for you to write down the girls' specialists' information so that you also have it. Dr. Campalattaro is Navah's ophthalmologist. Here is his number and address. She has a follow-up appointment in 6 months. Dr. Wolf is Kaya's neurologist. This is his number, and she has an appointment next month."

He started crying and said, "Amore, I am so sorry that I am not home to help you with the girls."

"Ed, please, you are my number one priority. Please don't worry. I will take care of the girls!"

More than ever, I wanted to be by Ed's side. I knew that he was feeling lonely. I was upset that I had to wait for the family leave, and I needed help with the girls. I took all the babysitting help that was offered to me by my friends, relatives, neighbors, and parents in my daughter's school community. I also got creative in finding ways to keep the girls occupied and cared for. During a talent show, the other parents jumped at the opportunity to watch the girls. I arranged playdates, which allowed the girls to be supervised while spending time with friends. I did all that I could to find more time with Ed.

On the days I was unable to find care for the girls, I could not see Ed. When this happened, I felt guilty, angry, and sad. One day, I felt this urge to go see Ed, but it was late. I couldn't shake the feeling that I had to see him. I called my sister, Glenny, and asked her to please come and stay overnight in our apartment with the girls. I wanted to be able to stay at the hospital with Ed.

Ed was feeling down and discouraged and needed emotional support. I was incredibly grateful that Glenny agreed to stay with the girls. This was the first night that I had slept away from my daughters. That night, I experienced the cruel reality of what Ed's life had become. He did not have the opportunity to have any consistent rest as he was constantly woken up for uncomfortable tests and health checks.

By the morning, I was sobbing. I told Ed, "I am so sorry that you are going through this. I wish I could stay here with you every day."

For bonus material go to ...

Out of nowhere, he also responded through tears, "Do you agree that losing Kai was so hard, but what I am going through is even harder?"

"Yes," I replied in a soft voice, feeling his pain. It tore me apart to see him like that. Every part of me wished I could fix it, that I could take his pain away and have a normal life again.

When Caring People Come Together, Miracles Happen

I went home that day and called my brother, Endy. Both Ed and the girls needed me, and I couldn't be in two places at once.

"Good morning, Endy. How are you?"

"I am doing well, but more importantly, how are you? I have been thinking of you and Ed and the girls."

"In all honesty, I don't know what to do. Ed needs me. He seems so down, and I feel like he is giving up and somehow detaching... But I have no one to watch the girls. With Mom away, the best I can do is take the help from the community when it's available, but it's not always reliable. I am feeling torn. I just wish I could catch a break."

"You know, I might have someone who can help. Do you remember Marlene, who is as beautiful as a ruby? She is a girl I told you about a few years ago."

"Yes, I kind of remember."

"We have been talking again. Jay, when I spoke with her last, she offered to come from Florida to New York City to help you. She'll stay with you to be there for the girls, so that you can be with Ed. She is sweet and kind and also has a daughter who is close in age to your girls."

He went on to say, "She is waiting for her daughter to get her visa and move to America. She can stay with you until Ed comes home."

I felt really good about my conversation with Endy and, the next day, I visited Ed and shared this information. He thought it was a great idea. He seemed to brighten up, which made me happier than I had felt in weeks. I called Endy right from Ed's side.

"Ed and I would love her help!"

Marlene arrived March 3rd, 2019, and I immediately felt a great sense of relief. She was exactly as my brother described: a loving and positive young woman. And he was right; she was as beautiful as a ruby! So much so, that Ruby became her nickname. I was very thankful for her kindness. She began picking up the girls from after-care, and I no longer needed to rush out of the hospital.

Ed and I enjoyed talking to each other and just spending time together. He would update me on his most current results and pending tests. I was able to be present when the doctors did their rounds. This was incredibly important as they always provided important information and discussed the next steps.

Denial

On March 4th, I arrived at the hospital and greeted the familiar nurses, feeling light and positive. Just before I entered his room, one of his doctors met with me and said, "Mrs. Jalowiecki, I want to speak with you."

I felt the lightness being quickly replaced by a heavy feeling of sadness.

"I want you to hope for the best, but plan for the worst."

"What do you mean?"

"Ed's health is deteriorating. He is not responding to the current treatment plan. His fevers are ongoing, so we had to postpone his transplant. These are all signs that we need to pay attention to. I know that you are very hopeful, but you also need to face reality."

I felt the anger erupt in me before I could stop it.

"You can tell me whatever you want, but I know that God has the last word!"

I walked away and, instead of going to Ed's room, I went to the restroom, kneeled down, and started praying and crying. I did this for a while until someone knocked on the door. I got up, cleaned my face, and touched up my makeup.

I entered Ed's room with a big smile, filled with hope and love, and said, "Hello, amore, look at you; you look so handsome today! I am so happy to be here with you. I brought a pink drink for you!"

He gave me a big smile and thanked me for the drink and for the visit. At this point, I was overwhelmed by thoughts and feelings of uncertainty and anguish. Deep inside, I was scared and very worried. Yet, I was hopeful that somehow Ed's health was going to turn around and he was going to get better.

On March 5th, Dr. Jurcic, who was sensitive and kind, met with me and said, "Nancy, I think that you should request your family leave now. We are no longer recommending that you wait until April. Ed needs you now."

I went to work the next day, spoke with my principal, Ms. Rodriguez, and her secretary, Ms. Zavala, and submitted the request for my family leave starting the following week on Monday, March 11th. I got the application approved on Thursday, March 7th, and my last day at work was Friday, March 8th. I remember going to the hospital right after work that day and sharing the wonderful news with Ed.

He said, "Amore, why don't you wait?"

Knowing that Ed needed me right away and not wanting to debate it with him, I replied, "You don't tell me what to do anymore!"

For bonus material go to ...

He smiled and said, "You always do what you want anyway."

I smiled back. I spent my whole afternoon and evening with Ed. He had a cup of vegetable broth, and I had Thai food for dinner. It was great! I gave him the head, hand, and feet massages that he loved so much.

On Saturday, March 9th, I went to the hospital bright and early.

I had been postponing this conversation. However, with the new information Dr. Jurcic had shared with me, I knew I had to ask the question. "Ed, is there anything you want me to know or share just in case things don't go as planned?"

He looked at me for a moment. "Do you think I am not going to make it?"

"It's not that. I just want you to know that I am here to listen and that you can talk to me about anything you wish."

He simply replied, "If something happens to me, Kaya and Navah will be with you, and if anything happens to you, they will both go with Mark and Elba. That is what we agreed on, right?"

"Yes, that's the plan."

I continued to be optimistic, but the harsh reality was staring right at me.

Facing the Reality and Not Feeling Prepared

On March 11th, I arrived at the hospital, and I was informed that one of the physician assistants (PA) wanted to speak with me. When I met with him, he shared that he was recommending that I seek palliative care for Ed. He felt that the palliative care team could help in providing more care options for Ed, to make him comfortable in the end-of-life process.

Reluctantly, I replied, "If this is the recommendation, we will do it." At this point, I was seeing what I did not want to see. But I was still hopeful. I was visualizing Ed fever free, getting his transplant, and coming home to a celebration.

He added that the team would be giving Ed more flexibility to enjoy the little things that hospital restrictions had prevented him from experiencing prior. This included things like helping him go outside to enjoy a sunset, go home for a few days, or have people visit him. Although these new opportunities were wonderful, this also meant planning for when things went downhill.

Shortly after my conversation with the PA, I entered Ed's room. His room was the last one at the end of the hallway. I did not like it. It was lonely and the last to get serviced. I entered the room and did not say anything to Ed about the PA's recommendations.

Ed was quiet and distant and was dealing with stomach discomfort. After the last round of chemotherapy, he had a stroke and his intestines were compromised, causing two air pockets to develop. He could no longer eat or drink at this point.

For bonus material go to ...

Ed's physical therapist came in the room and reminded Ed that he should take a walk. He did not feel like walking or exercising, but together, holding arms, we were able to walk around the unit. Ed was fragile, pale, and tired. For the first time, he asked me for help when taking a shower. I said, "Ed, please think positively and visualize yourself healing and in good health!"

"Amore, it's not my mind but my body giving up on me," he responded despondently.

In the evening of March 12th, a nasal feeding tube was inserted. I called Ed shortly after the procedure and asked him how he was doing.

"It was a terrible experience. This is so uncomfortable."

"I am coming back to be with you tonight."

"You've been here twice today; you don't have to come back."

"I want to," I responded.

I arrived at the hospital and Ed shared his experience with the nasal feeding tube procedure. I felt awful that he had to go through so much pain and discomfort, and that all our hopes for the transplant were vanishing.

Three days on ice chips, no drinks or food, and he now had a nasal tube that was extracting air and fluids. His stomach was swollen, and he could hardly move. His feet were swollen, and he was in extreme discomfort. We were up all night. There was one complication after another. And then a large oxygen tank was brought into the room. He was not getting enough oxygen. Despite all of this, he still looked strong and determined.

At around 6:30 a.m., I called an Uber and got home quickly. I made myself a cup of coffee and then got in the shower, and as I was getting dressed, one of the physician assistants called me.

"Hi, Jay."

"Hi, is Ed okay?" I replied.

"I know you just left, but we need you to come back to the hospital as soon as possible." I hung up the phone with shaking hands and finished getting dressed.

I returned to the hospital to find his room full of staff. One of Ed's air pockets had erupted. Since he no longer had a functioning immune system, they couldn't take the risk of operating on him. The surgeon felt that they would lose him on the operating table. He was already taking morphine to help him deal with the pain. The only option was transferring him to the intensive care unit.

My brother, Endy, got to the hospital at that moment. The PA had called him since he was my emergency contact. We moved to the ICU. They asked me to wait in a room nearby while they changed Ed to a hospital gown. When I came back to the room, Ed shared that it was a horrible experience because they had to move him around and he was in so much pain. He was so fragile that something as simple as getting dressed was excruciating.

For bonus material go to ...

I met with Dr. Flores from the palliative care unit. She asked me to reach out to Kaya and Navah's school and have someone bring them to the hospital to see their daddy.

Everything was happening so fast.

A child therapist saw the girls when they arrived, to prepare them emotionally. She spoke to them about their daddy being in the hospital for some time but not getting better. Navah was really upset and went under a chair for a few minutes. The therapist brought some materials so that the girls could each create a special wooden box to place things that reminded them of their daddy.

Once the session was completed, both girls and I went to see Ed. They both started asking him many questions, and he answered each one of them. When he was finished answering, Kaya hugged his left leg. He held Kaya's hand in his left hand and Navah's hand in his right.

"I love you both so much. You will always be in my heart, and Daddy will always be with you."

I cried. It touched me so deeply to see how brave my husband was. Shortly after this moment, the girls left with Ruby and Endy.

The Magical Shimmering Glow

When I saw Ed's soul leaving his body, it was the most powerful yet desperate moment of my life. I felt as if part of me was leaving with him, and somehow, I was no longer whole. I could not stop crying and hugging his body.

"If I knew that you were going to die anyway, I would have taken you out of here and enjoyed kissing and hugging you. I would not have restricted our daughters from doing the same."

I continued hugging and speaking to Ed for a while; it was just what I felt like doing. My mom and my brother, Pedro, were there. Ed's doctor came in and I saw him cry too. Shortly after, there was a parade of nurses. Ed had developed such a wonderful relationship with his doctor and nurses. He was always thankful to them, and they felt his love and gratitude.

The World Keeps Moving and YOU Can't Stop It

At this point, I was devastated, overwhelmed, and sad. Ed had just passed a few minutes earlier. I was still trying to hold on to his body. I did not want to stop talking about how unfair it was that he was without food or water for several days. If he was going to die anyway, why did I allow this to happen?

Shortly after Ed's passing, I was also being asked to share the news with Ed's mom, who had just arrived after missing a bus, and who was looking forward to seeing her son. In that moment, I had to prepare myself to share the news with her in a gentle, caring way. I wanted to protect her from the pain, the devastating pain of not being there to say the last goodbye.

I collected myself and greeted her. "I am so sorry that you missed the bus. I am so sorry that I was not able to pick you up at the bus terminal."

For bonus material go to ...

The first thing she said was, "Where is my son?"

I shared the terrible news.

She screamed, "It took me 11 years to conceive my son, and leukemia comes and takes him in five months."

Ed was her only child and the product of fertility treatments and a lot of persistence from his parents.

I remember being asked to leave the room because Ed's body needed to be transported to the morgue. I was told I should follow up with a funeral home and make the arrangements. I thanked Dr. Flores and I asked for more time with Ed's body. I was granted a few more precious moments alone with Ed. I looked around the room... I wanted to see if I would see his soul glowing somewhere in the room, but it was gone.

I took some time to just look at him—his body, his hands, his feet, his face—I don't really know why. I just didn't want to leave him. I held his feet in my hands and said, "I enjoyed massaging these feet."

Ed used to tell me, "When you massage my feet, it is such a treat. Thank you, amore!"

This time, I could hear his voice, just like he could hear my voice when I was not around... suddenly, I gave up. I knew I had to go home to my daughters without him and share the news one more time.

www.griefandgratitudebook.com

My brother Pedro, my mom, my cousin Damaris, and one of my chosen sisters in this life, Francia, were there with me. And our hearts were sad, and our hugs were tight. Telling Kaya, who was seven, and Navah, who was five that their daddy had gone to heaven was one of the hardest moments of all.

Thank You

Thank you for reading the story of my husband's transition from this life. I felt it was important to share more in detail just how difficult those days were for me, because I know I am not alone. Most people go into the hospital and leave in a day or two or maybe a week. It is a very different experience when you have a loved one in the hospital for months, and for some of you, for years. During that time, you may feel as though your purpose is to care for others, and it is often hard to think of yourself and what you need. You still have needs, even though you are the last person that you are thinking about.

The difficult part after you lose a loved one is to remember to break that pattern. You do get to live again. You do get to dream again. You are worthy of more love in your life.

For bonus material go to ...

I am Affirmations

Try writing out these affirmations and feel their power within you:

I am strength.
I am love.
I am light.
I am worthy of happiness.
I welcome joy in my life.

As you write out this affirmation, take notice of your thoughts. Do you believe what you are writing? If not, keep going. Write it again and again and again. Journal about your worthiness. If you have any other thoughts that you would like to share, please write them below.

_____
_____
_____
_____
_____

www.griefandgratitudebook.com

My Notes

For bonus material go to www.griefandgratitudebook.com

My Notes

Chapter 3
Walking into the Unknown

"When you walk to the edge of all the light you have and take that first step into the darkness of the unknown, you must believe that one of two things will happen. There will be something solid for you to stand upon or you will be taught to fly."
– Patrick Overton

3

Trust me when I tell you that with time, you will feel better. That statement may make you want to close this book, because you have heard others say it before and you just do not believe it. It may feel as though the darkness that has enveloped you in this moment will stay forever. It won't. The light will find a way to break through.

You will feel better one day. Keep moving. Keep living because you will build a new life for yourself and your children, if you have them. I understand that if you are going through the emotional pain and dealing with the devastating circumstances of losing a loved one, it's hard for you to see past your current reality. My intention in writing this book is that you will gain some tools to apply to your own experience with grief, and these tools can help you see the light on the darkest of days.

Your grief is part of your new reality, and an experience that you need to go through for your soul to heal and evolve. It's important to remember at this moment that you may feel stuck in a deep valley or as though you are going through a dark tunnel alone, but if you keep walking forward, you will find your way out again. Remember, you are not stuck in the valley; you are going through it and starting a new journey and It is a new chapter even though it may feel like one that you are not up for. This is normal, and it is perfectly okay to feel this way. The best thing about experiencing this chapter of your life, is that you will do things that you never thought you could. This is a time in your life when you are vulnerable, yet strong and resilient.

In this chapter, I want to share with you some of the things I experienced following Ed's death. While I had experienced grief with the loss of our baby, this was something new and entirely different. Not only that, but the world keeps on moving, and I had to learn how to keep moving with it. During this time, as life drove forward, I often felt like it was dragging me along with it, and I was holding on by the ends of my fingertips.

Feeling the Loneliness

When it started sinking in that Ed was no longer coming home, I felt a lingering feeling of loneliness. I did my best at first to push it aside. It hurt too much. It was like having a herniated disk pressing on the sciatic nerve. The pain never went away, and it was excruciating. It was this ever-present feeling that I could not shake no matter how hard I tried. There were moments when I felt it less. Then, unexpectedly, it would come shooting back again, piercing my heart.

Ed was such a major part of my life, and there was so much love in my heart for what we had created. I felt his loss so deeply. I remember many days when I would look at the clock and know exactly what we would be doing if he was still here. When this happened, it would lead me back to the memories I held so close to my heart. I would let them play and replay in my mind. I would cry and think about his humor, sarcasm, kindness, intellect, and strength.

This may happen to you as well, and it's all normal. Just let it be and it will pass. Release and surrender to the moment. However, if you feel that this keeps happening for long periods of time and you cannot get out of it, try turning your thoughts to some things you are grateful for in the moment. Listening to music or going for a walk can also help. I would say something like this to myself: "I am so grateful for all these great memories of my husband. Amore, you were a blessing in my life. I am a better person because of you." In that moment, I felt gratitude in my heart.

This thought would make me smile. There were times when I used this same affirmation of gratitude to help me get out of bed in the mornings on the days when it was difficult. I would then smile, rinse my face, put on some makeup, and get out for fresh air and a cup of tea or coffee at a local café. Sometimes I would put on my sneakers and go for a walk at the Cloisters, a nearby park in my community. Believe it or not, this really helped in refocusing my thoughts and elevating my energy.

When loneliness feels unbearable, find some things to do to help you get out of it. Is there a good friend you can call to meet you for a chat and a coffee? If you do not feel like talking with anyone, maybe there is a nature path you can visit or a city street with shops you enjoy looking in. It is important in these moments to be kind to yourself and to take care of your needs. Your needs matter!

For bonus material go to ...

Complicated Grief

For some people, feelings of loss are debilitating and don't improve even after time passes. This is known as complicated grief, sometimes called persistent complex bereavement disorder. In complicated grief, painful emotions are so long-lasting and severe that you have trouble recovering from the loss and resuming your own life.

Different people follow different paths through the grieving experience. The order and timing of these phases may vary from person to person:

- Accepting the reality of your loss
- Allowing yourself to experience the pain of your loss
- Adjusting to a new reality in which the deceased is no longer physically present
- Having other relationships

These differences are normal. However, if you're unable to move through these stages for more than a year after the death of a loved one, you may have complicated grief.

At one point during my experience with grief, I began entertaining the kind of grief that affects a small percentage of people who experience the loss of a loved one. I was filled with a kind of anger I had never felt in my life before. It was one that made me question everything about Ed's death.

I had decided that something must have gone wrong because Ed could not have died otherwise. He was too strong. He was too healthy before his diagnosis. I wanted to prove that the medication that Ed was using for eight months caused his cancer.

I was so serious about these allegations that I started planning the next steps to do this. It was kind of like my own scientific research project. I decided that I would go for a thorough medical examination first. I wanted to get a full understanding of what my starting place was, what my baseline was. I would then begin taking the same medication Ed had been taking to treat the wart on his left foot. Yes, you did read that correctly. I believed his wart medication ultimately caused his death, and I was willing to take my chances and get leukemia too to prove my theory right.

I thought that if I lost my life in the process, it was not a big deal; I would just be closer to Ed. These were the thoughts of complicated grief, which was something I didn't know existed as I was going through it.

I was not talking to anyone about this at the time. Luckily, I had Alison, Ed's social worker, who reached out and informed me of the Healing Hearts Bereavement Retreat and encouraged me to apply. Even though a part of me did not want to do this, I worried that I would let Alison down. She had done so much for my beloved Ed, as well as for myself and our children when we needed her the most.

She was the person who arranged our "sharing a meal with Daddy visits" for us. During this time, Kaya and Navah and I would go to the hospital and eat with Ed. These were some of my better memories from the time he was in the hospital, and I was so grateful to Alison for facilitating these moments. So, I applied

For bonus material go to ...

and waited and then got a call from Claire! As you know, I was one of the families that received a spot where everything was paid for to attend the Healing Hearts Retreat with the girls. Once I found out we got the spot, I had homework to do. The girls and I had to prepare by gathering some of Ed's things to honor him at the retreat. I also had to write a biography about Ed. This homework saved me in a way. It took me out of my anger and gave me a more positive goal surrounding Ed's life and death.

I started to reflect and write Ed's biography, and I had to stop at one point because I could not stop crying. Then, the next day, I would go back to write some more, and the same thing would happen. This went on for several days. Finally, I finished! I read it over one last time and felt a feeling of love and admiration for Ed, who was such a beautiful soul. I once again was able to feel that gratitude for what we had created together. Writing that biography brought back the feeling of love. I was feeling good.

I was once again able to perform my everyday activities and went back to work. Both of these were signs that I had made it back into a healthy grieving process.

If you are experiencing feelings of blame, guilt, or lingering thoughts that your life has no purpose, or wishing that you were the one who died, please seek professional help. You can start with a social worker, your doctor, or a therapist, who can refer you or provide the support you need. Or you can reach out to CancerCare. This incredible organization will provide you with amazing support.

Dealing with the Finances

After the passing of a spouse, it can be stressful dealing with your finances. Sometimes you may think, "If only the world would stop turning for just a moment while I figure this out." Many of your monthly financial obligations will always be there no matter what the circumstances are. The bank will still want the mortgage payments on time. The phone bills need to be paid. The kids need to eat. Although you may feel that everything in your world has been completely turned upside down, some things have not; they just seem a bit heavier to carry.

In my case, and since Ed was very organized, he used to manage our finances. He always planned ahead of time for our vacations and outings. However, two months before his passing, he said, "Amore, I now wish to transfer our online account to a physical account, where you will have total access to our money."

He made an appointment at the bank that was located on the first floor of the hospital, and we met with a manager and opened a joint account. Ed had also contacted the Social Security office and completed the application and made an appointment for an interview over the phone for the month of April. Due to Ed's proactive planning, after his passing, the Social Security office called me. All I had to do was confirm all the information Ed had previously provided. Ed did his best to make it as easy for me as possible after he was gone.

Unlike me, I know of so many people whose spouses or partners managed the finances, and they had a complete lack of knowledge about how to manage them after losing their loved ones. They had no idea what resources were available to them or how to manage the debt they had. They had no life insurance or were not listed as a beneficiary on a pension. The learning curve can be steep if you were not the one to manage your family finances, or maybe your spouse/partner did not leave you in the best of situations. It can feel like an overwhelming burden when you do not feel like you have the energy to take on anything more.

In many cases, there is no other option but to start from scratch. If this is your situation, I can only imagine how hard this is on you, but I am not able to truly put myself in your shoes. That said, here is a friendly reminder about a few things you can do to make dealing with the financial burden of the loss of your partner a little easier:

- Talk to a family member that you trust about what you need help with.
- Talk to your financial institution or a financial adviser.
- Reach out to a non-for-profit organization that is willing to assist families in need of help with funeral expenses and/or childcare.

I know that these chores may be the last thing you want to do, but they need your attention. If you wait too long to get a handle on your finances, it will just become more overwhelming. You can prioritize tasks of higher importance, like getting funding for the funeral, and then choose one task per day to tackle after that. This way, you make it easier to manage both the learning curve and everything that needs to get done.

For myself, I recall writing reminders down in a calendar that I kept with me at all times so that I would not forget any payment. While Ed did leave me in a good place, there was still a lot to do and to remember. Dealing with your financial situation, even at the best of times, can be stressful. At the worst of times, it can be almost unbearable. Give yourself a break and find every way possible to make it easier for you!

Sharing Your New Story

After losing Ed, I felt the need to talk about him, his illness, and the hospital experience. I found this to be one of the hardest things for me to do. I did not feel that there were many people who were able to give me what I needed, and it often made me angry. There were the people who wanted to talk too much, and I found this overwhelming. There were the people who avoided the subject altogether, as if Ed had never existed in my life. There were the people who would patiently listen as I talked, and they would sometimes offer their opinions. But often, their feedback made me angry. I disliked it when someone would say, "He's in a better place now."

I wanted to scream: "NO, HE IS NOT! I am here. His daughters are here. His life is here! There is no better place than being with us, HERE."

Also, if I heard, "I'm sorry for your loss," one more time, I felt like I was going to lose it. Of course, people were sorry, but what does that even really mean? How did it help me to hear it?

For bonus material go to ...

As time went on, I quickly learned that people mean well and that they may not know what to say. This is when I learned not to take any encounters personally. Maybe I did similar things in the past, but now I know better, so I do better.

When I would run into someone in public who knew both Ed and me, just after he was gone, the sight of that person often brought me to tears, and not silently. Sometimes, I could not stop myself from openly sobbing. Many times, I could not even bring myself to speak. There was nothing I could do at that moment but let go. I didn't care who was looking or what they were thinking. I didn't care what the response of the person I had run into was.

Life can be messy and uncomfortable. Let yourself cry in public if you need to. Don't worry about what others think. Sometimes, even now I still tear up, but I've gotten past the stage of breaking down completely. I still don't feel bad though, and I never will for sharing my emotional response to my grief with others in my life. I think the thing to always remember when talking about your reality with others is that there is no right response. Give your loved ones a break here too. They mean well and want to give you comfort.

The Importance of Staying Healthy

"Good health is not something we can buy. However, it can be an extremely valuable savings account."
– Anne Wilson Schaef

When you are caring for a family member who has an illness, it's easy to go for long hours without nourishment. You may be so worried that you may even lose your appetite. During the time that Ed was in the hospital, I actually lost weight, not intentionally, but because of all the running around.

There was a Green Juice Café not too far from our apartment, and I used to go and grab a green juice, or a smoothie with fruits and protein, or a treat with a coffee. I also used to grab a salad to go. I took my vitamins every day and would carry fruits, protein bars, nuts, and water with me.

Providing my body with the nutrition that it needed was critical in maintaining my overall health and vitality when I was caring for Ed, not only while he was still alive but also after his passing. Consciously choosing healthy foods, especially when eating out more often, would help in sustaining your energy and in promoting your well-being.

One of the other things I did to ensure I wasn't missing anything in my own health was to ask for a checkup every six months rather than a year, especially during the toughest times. I suggest you do the same. Studies show that the risk of death increases for the surviving partner after the first few months of bereavement. You have heard the biblical phrase, "Treat your body as your temple." It's the only body you have. You may not feel like it right now, since I imagine you have put the care of someone else before yourself for a while now, but your health matters, and you are worthy of living a healthy life.

For bonus material go to ...

Stay Social!

I went from being married to being a single widow in what felt like the blink of an eye. It felt confusing at times. I had to adjust to my new family unit, which did not include Ed. I was not used to this. It was hard at first. Being social without your partner can actually do the opposite of what you think it might at first. It can actually contribute to your loneliness, because you will see others out with their partners. This is normal. Push through it, because one day you will want to socialize again, and it is easier if you have maintained your current relationships. Perhaps, like me, you will have the opportunity to build new ones with people who have gone through a similar experience.

That said, it was also important for me to express my feelings and to say *no* if I did not want to accept an invitation. Or if I really wasn't sure, I took my time to give a response by saying, "Thank you so much for thinking of me and for the invitation. I am not sure at this moment but will let you know soon if I can join you."

One thing that I really enjoyed was meeting with my friends on a one-to-one basis. Some of my fondest memories from just after Ed died were meeting with my friend, Elba, at Floridita, and another day with Judy, at Mambi restaurant. I remember enjoying our conversations about life, love, and healing. Their hugs uplifted my soul. When I got home, I felt better for having gone.

Do what feels right. And when you feel like doing nothing, just do nothing. It is a balancing act. Sometimes thinking of what is best for your self-care means staying in, and sometimes it means going out. Start to really listen to yourself. Get in tune with what you need physically, emotionally, and spiritually.

Being There for Others

I remember talking to my friend, Francia, and learning that her husband, Alex, ended up in the hospital the same day Ed passed. She had left Alex and came to the hospital to be there for me. She did not share what was going on with Alex, not wanting to put more on my plate. Three days later. Alex passed. I remember us calling and checking up on each other. She came to Ed's funeral, and I went to Alex's. Here we were, my best friend and I, going through the same thing at the same time.

Being there for Francia was comforting as I was not alone. I also wanted her to know that I was there for her regardless of what I was going through. I could relate to how she was feeling.

Being there for her was saying: "I am here with you. It's painful and it hurts, but here is my shoulder and I know I have yours."

Perhaps you know of a friend, a neighbor, or someone you cared about who has also lost a loved one. Knowing exactly how they feel, you can be a great comfort to them.

Get Help, Find Community

Be open and welcome all the help that is offered to you and your children after the loss of a loved one. I felt so much love and

For bonus material go to ...

received a great deal of help from my school community, PS 98, the girls' school community of Muscota, and from their after-school program, Be Me.

    PS 98, was extraordinarily supportive, flexible, and generous during this time. When I think of them, I can find no words to truly describe how much they gave to me, other than to thank them from the bottom of my heart. I wish this for you too. I hope that you are able to surround yourself with a community of people whose support will also fill your heart with gratitude. If you feel you do not have this now, how can you find one? Is there a social worker you can speak with to help you find the right group? You need people to help you through this time. Do not go through it alone!

    For me, there was also Alli and Camille, from Mascota. They contacted me on behalf of the school. The girls were being provided with therapy at the school and they had initiated a Go Fund Me page for us. Kaya and Navah's teachers, Susana, Marilyn, and Jean provided the girls with love and emotional support. They all wanted to know how else they could help my family. I thanked them for their ongoing love and kindness. I was very lucky to be part of such a caring, supportive, and loving school community.

    Ali, one of the administrators, also wanted to know if I was open to meeting with a school community member who had also lost her husband to cancer. The community member was a mother too, and Alli thought it might be helpful to meet and ask questions about how she dealt with losing her husband. I agreed and met with her at a nearby coffee shop. She was open and honest with me. We had a positive conversation. I remember asking her many questions and learning that she was engaged and experiencing love again. It gave me hope.

Katherine, the program coordinator, and Victoria, one of the social workers from the Be Me after-school program, called to check up on me as well. I met with them both and was impressed by their kindness. I had a session with Victoria, and she listened and passed me a box of tissues as I could not stop crying. She provided me with community resources and printed out information about the stages of grieving, which I read and found helpful.

She also informed me of an art therapy class that she thought was going to be beneficial for the girls during this time and beyond. She had coordinated for Kaya and Navah to attend the Twelve Trails summer camp at no cost to us. This program was an amazing opportunity for the girls to be in an educational open space. They got to spend time with friends, create, and be in touch with nature, swim, and have fun.

I was overwhelmed by Victoria's kindness and the program's generosity. She gave me a big hug, and all I could say was *thank you!*

Be Kind to Yourself, the Only You There Is

My desire for you, as you read this chapter, is that you know just how important it is to take care of yourself during a difficult time of your life. This is not only for you but also for your family. A big part of taking care of yourself is understanding the challenges you are facing, not only in grief but also in the normal day-to-day activities in life. Take some reflection time to understand what you do and do not need socially, and how you can find a community of support.

After Ed's passing, I realized that I needed to feel 100% present for my daughters, who were depending on me to have their needs met. Life kept moving and, at times, I felt that I had hardly any time to just BE. I craved time to just be with me. That's right! Then I started becoming more aware of my needs. If I felt like being in the shower a little longer, I did this. If a song came to mind and I wanted to sing it, I would search for it and sing. Listening to music and closing my eyes was reenergizing.

Being kind to yourself is something that I can't stress enough, because it's the last thing that you think about after losing a loved one. Too many things are happening all at once. You may have to learn new skills. You may have to adjust to being a single parent. You may have a harder time navigating social situations alone. You have to learn how to say *no* or to say *yes* again.

There is no right or wrong way of feeling. Remember to always be kind to yourself. Give yourself a big hug and smile and say, "I am grateful that I am here and can feel this hug." Tell yourself, "I love you," and hold yourself tight.

www.griefandgratitudebook.com

Affirmation

In each chapter, I will come back to these affirmations because they can be a good tool in harnessing the power of your thoughts, especially in heartbreaking times.

Try writing out these affirmations:

I am grateful for myself.
I love me and all that I am.
I am thankful for my life.

As you write out this affirmation, take notice of your thoughts. Do you believe what you are writing? If not, keep going. Write it again and again and again. Write all about why you love yourself and how great you are! Connect with the feeling of gratitude and feel appreciation for who you are.

_____
_____
_____
_____
_____

For bonus material go to www.griefandgratitudebook.com

My Notes

Chapter 4
Life Is Everything

"No one saves us but ourselves. No one can and no one may. We ourselves must walk the path."
– Gautama Buddha

4

Shortly after Ed's passing and as life hit harder than I had ever imagined it could, I began to feel like a wild bird thrown into a cage. I was hurting, sad, lonely, and filled with uncertainty and fear. There were many things that just did not go as planned for my family. However, as time passed, I came to the realization that I was not alone and that other individuals and families shared a similar experience with me.

My Grief, My Ally

Through my process with grief, I learned that in order to experience everything in life again, I had to make a choice. It was up to me and no one else to take control of my life and decide whether I was going to live again and move my daughters forward in life. By this, I mean truly living, allowing the grief to become a part of me and set me free. I needed to let loose and fly again even when my wings felt too fragile. I was alive and knew that I must rise again. Yes, some days were so hard I could barely move, but this is my grief, my new friend. I had to face life, but this time with it by my side, and experience the lows and the highs. We as one had to get up and fly through the big blue sky, and also through the clouds, both big and small, dense and light, on sunny or stormy days.

For me, the desire to fly away kept coming back to me. I needed adventure again, even with the pain. I needed to get excited about my life; not only for me but for my young daughters. This meant travel, prayer, meditation, mindfulness and yoga. For you, the ways in which you rise up and fly again will be different. You might want to get back to some of the things you used to love to do before, like volunteering, creating art, or going to the gym regularly. Or you might want to go back to school and embark on a whole different kind of adventure. As you read this chapter, think about what lights you up. Dream big and then dream even bigger. Turn your dreams into goals! Smile more, breathe and get excited about life.

Transforming Grief into Courage

Grief has a never-ending flow. It is like a river flowing into the ocean. Sometimes the rapids pull you along so fast you cannot catch your breath. Sometimes you float, and sometimes you are the one who needs to take charge and swim to calmer waters. Once you hit the ocean, you know that some days you will encounter storms, but in your journey, you have gathered strength. Recognize that you are resilient. With time, you will develop a better sense of direction and where you are meant to go.

This ocean is a place where my grief had transformed my fears into courage and, therefore, helped me move through life, supporting both myself and my daughters. I was able to summon this courage to overcome my fears and to continue to carry out the dreams and goals Ed and I had for Kaya and Navah. I continue to integrate his values, beliefs, morals, passions, and vision into their lives. His energy, love, and endless memories are integrated into the courage that fills my life as I move forward.

Ready or Not, Life Keeps Going

Taking a solo retreat was an idea that came to mind after losing control one night and getting very upset in front of the girls. I just missed Ed so much. Kaya ran to her room crying. I knew she was feeling the loss of her daddy. She was the oldest and had a special bond with him. Living without Ed was particularly difficult for her.

One day, Navah grabbed my face and stared at me intently. She looked at me through tear-filled eyes and said, "Mommy, look at me. I look just like Daddy. When you are crying because you miss Daddy, look at me and think of Daddy."

"You're right, Navah. Mommy will do just that next time she misses Daddy."

This was when I felt in my heart that I needed to be alone in order to grieve. I needed time to feel the pain and just let it out without reservations.

I was also very worried. I was worried about the girls. I was worried about myself. I was worried about us as a family unit. I was worried about everything. But more than that, I was in search of answers. Why did Ed have to leave us so soon? What would I do as a single mom? What was the purpose of my life? What would help me to become stronger?

For bonus material go to ...

I had this desire to detach from everyone and everything I loved too. There was a part of me that felt like it wasn't fair for Ed to have had to say goodbye to Kaya and Navah so soon in his life, and I was able to continue watching them grow. My thoughts and emotions were complicated, but the one thing I felt was an unwavering desire to be with myself—to be alone to figure my new reality out. It was clear in my mind that I needed to feel good in order to be able to support the emotional needs my daughters had.

I started to plan what I now refer to as my solo retreat. For some reason, it was Asia that was calling to me. *Thailand and Japan are the countries I will visit*, I thought. *Thailand is a spiritual place filled with spiritual rituals and is on the other side of the world.*

Thailand, for me, became a place to finally go within. I could cry, scream, yell, and get as upset as I needed to without worrying about who might see or hear me. I could also pray and meditate and heal my heart. Or at least try. I wanted to visit the Golden Buddha to ask for guidance and clarity, and to find a way to reconnect with my soul. The Golden Buddha is the biggest Buddha statue made of solid gold. This was not known until 1955, when it was being relocated and the plaster was chipped off and the gold revealed. I wanted to visit its temple as it represented something greater to see and connect with. I do believe that the traumatic experiences that you and I have experienced have helped us in discovering our true potential that was hidden deep inside us. For now, we realize our strength and worthiness and can consciously allow the sun to shine upon us again.

Japan was my next stop because I had always wanted to learn more about Japanese culture and language. I took Japanese in high school. I enjoyed the way the teacher used to speak to us about the culture, and I was fascinated by the language. She often talked about the Japanese gardens and how spiritual and peaceful they were. The pictures she showed us were beautiful. I thought, "What a marvelous place to visit one day." My day had come because on my list of places to see in this world was Kamikatsu, a town in Shikoku, Japan. Online, inadvertently, I found this pristine town in line with nature, when I was inspired to do some research.

One morning, I was speaking with Maru, one of our custodians, and I said, "Maru, do we recycle here? I noticed that everything goes to the same trash can, except for paper."

"Yes, we do. But we could always do better."

"Do you think we can become a zero-waste school?"

"Anything is possible!"

So, I began searching for ways to initiate a zero-waste program in my school community. In this search, I came across the beautiful town of Kamikatsu, which at the time was known for its declaration to aim for zero waste by 2020. This inspired me and I knew I had to go there.

I contacted my traveling coordinator and learned that there was a layover in Hong Kong both ways. *Great,* I thought, *I could spend a few days there and see an old friend who I had not seen in years and who had reached out after Ed's passing.*

Once I decided that my solo retreat had to happen for my own healing, I started making real plans. I spoke with my colleague, Ms. Pena, and she provided me with some information about Thailand since she had been there. I spoke with my daughter's Japanese teacher and friend, Maki, about being my tour guide in Kamikatsu, since she was going to be in Japan at the time of my visit. Maki was very kind and helpful and coordinated our trip from Tokyo to Kamikatsu.

I spoke with Ruby, and she agreed to stay with the girls during my solo retreat. My mom had reached out because she wanted to spend some time with her granddaughters. She was crying and expressed feelings of guilt for not being around when I needed her the most. I shared my plans for the solo retreat and told her that if she wanted, she could come and stay with the girls and help Ruby out during the time that I was going to be away. She was happy to help.

I prepared a folder, with all the important documents: my employer, life insurance policy, pension information, my social security number, email, and passwords. Additionally, I added a copy of my will, stating what I wanted done with my belongings in case anything happened to me and I did not return. Furthermore, I added a copy of the document Ed and I had created, stating that if anything happened to me, the girls would be cared for by Elba, Kaya's godmother, and her husband, Mark, whom Ed called "my brother from another mother."

Everything was falling into place, and soon I would be able to just be alone and far from everything, but closer to Ed, closer to my grief, and most importantly, closer to God. This was a big part of what this trip was for me as well. I needed to be away from all of the other distractions. I wanted to allow my mind, body, and soul to go through the transformation I knew I needed since I was no longer the same.

At this time, it was April, and we had lived 5 weeks without Ed. I was back to work and living in my new reality. Navah's birthday was around the corner, and she had been looking forward to celebrating her 6th birthday with her daddy.

"Navah, what do you want to do for your birthday?" I asked her.

"Mommy, I want it to be just like my 4th birthday."

"Okay, I can do that!"

For a morning celebration at Bennett Park, I contacted Blue Balloon Parties and got the package with the bunny, and then everything was set. April 30th finally arrived. It was my first birthday without Ed.

My siblings, Mark and Elba, Francia, and other close friends gathered to celebrate Navah. We all talked about Ed and shared how much we missed him, but we also reminded each other to keep things about my beautiful daughter and her birthday. This was one of the days on which my feelings truly fluctuated, going back and forth from sad to happy throughout the day. I am not sure how it happened, but I felt Ed's energy around the entire day. That night, however, was rough for me, and even though I didn't think it was possible, I fell asleep in the company of my sorrow.

It was seven weeks since Ed's passing, and I was really having a hard time. Ed used to make such a big deal of Mother's Day. He always made me feel so special and loved. I remember thinking back and could almost smell the yummy breakfast being made for me: tofu with garlic, salted onions and cilantro sprinkled with curry, along with homemade potatoes and a delicious cup of cafe con leche.

I stayed in bed that morning just a little longer so that I could live in that memory. But soon enough, I got up and went to the park where I could watch the girls playing, running around, and talking to friends. This was one of the things Ed and I would have done if he was around. This was a way for me to feel closer to him.

As you may be aware by now, holidays and birthdays are triggers. Each time, especially early on, I relived the pain and sadness that Ed was not there to share these special moments in my life. Getting out and experiencing my new reality was sad, but it was also helpful in creating new memories. When you find the courage to go out of your home, you're giving yourself the opportunity to build new experiences. You are living in your reality rather than simply being dragged through it. It gave me some of my control back.

Eight weeks later, I could no longer bear to see our wedding photos up on the wall. I would look at the photos and feel a deep sadness take over me. I couldn't stop myself from crying. So, I decided to leave a collage of family photos from our last trip to the Dominican Republic at the entrance of our apartment, and I removed the other photos we had up in our living room, dining room, and bedroom. I found this simple change to be very helpful. But again, you may need to see pictures of your loved one all around. Go with what makes you feel good.

Healing and New Adventures

"Life always begins with one step outside of your comfort zone."
– Shannon L. Alder

It was time to make the final preparations for the two major events that were fast approaching: Healing Hearts Bereavement Retreat in June (which I've already shared with you), and shortly after that in July, I was finally leaving for 3 weeks, for my solo retreat to Asia!

On June 7th, I left work and picked up the rental car. Kaya and Navah were ready and waiting for me at home. I grabbed our bags and left at around 3:30 p.m. to go to Memorytown, Poconos, PA, where the Healing Hearts Retreat was taking place. I needed to be there before 7 p.m. Registration started at 5 p.m. Memorytown was a little over two hours from our New York City apartment. It was a beautiful sunny day, and leaving NYC was a piece of cake. However, shortly after leaving, we hit eight hours of traffic because of a terrible accident.

For bonus material go to ...

I almost turned around and went back home, but I could not let down the staff at Healing Hearts, who were waiting and kept checking up on us to make sure that we were okay. We arrived at the retreat after midnight.

The next morning, we were tired from our long journey. We got up slowly and got ready to go eat breakfast. I desperately needed a cup of coffee. As we crossed the street to go into the breakfast restaurant, we said good morning to a dad and a little girl. As we all walked through the front door, the staff greeted us and made sure that we were okay. The girls and I sat and had a warm and delicious breakfast. I looked around and realized how many other families had lost a loved one to cancer. I saw the children's faces reflected in my daughters'.

It was after breakfast this first morning when the girls first met Molly, and I let them play together while I set up our memory space for Ed. I watched the girls and I remember smiling. I knew there was a sadness there that I couldn't take away, but I was so proud of them at that moment—running and playing and enjoying life with a new friend, one they knew they could also help.

"Hi, my name is Mike. I am Molly's dad."

"Hi, my name is Nancy, and I am Kaya and Navah's mommy. Navah just told me that Molly lost her mommy and misses her so much!"

Mike got emotional.

"Yes," he managed to say. His eyes were watering. He brought his hand to his head and said, "Molly has not talked about her mom's passing with anyone, and the fact that she is talking to your daughter about her means the world to me."

I left Mike in the field with the girls and went to the loved ones memory table to set up for Ed. The space available for ours was next to where Mike had set up for Maria before coming to introduce himself.

I read her biography, which Mike had written, and tears came to my eyes. I started to think, Ed was forty-two and she was only thirty-five, even younger. Her daughters are younger than mine. She was so beautiful! Her smile was so bright and filled with life. After setting up for Ed, I spent a few minutes taking a look at the rest of the display on the long table. I looked at the pictures and read the biographies. I said a quick prayer and walked out of the room.

Back in the field, Mike met Kaya and Navah and I met Molly. Mike and I started to talk about Ed and Maria. We both got emotional. He shared that Molly's younger sister, Keeva, was at home with his parents. At this moment, the girls start running around and Molly and Kaya went in one direction, and Navah and another little girl went in another direction. So, Mike and I stopped sharing and agreed that he would follow Molly and Kaya and that I was going to follow Navah.

A few minutes later, we met again. While the girls were playing, we continued our conversation. This time, we spoke about

For bonus material go to ...

Ed and Maria's treatments, their stays at the hospital, and about the girls. We could not talk more than a few minutes at a time before we had to go in separate directions. It seemed that each conversation was cut short, and we could never finish discussing what we started.

When it was time to join our support group, Mike and I realized we were grouped together. As we walked to the meeting place, we both agreed that it was nice that the adults had some time together, without the children.

Our group had eight members and a counselor. Shortly after we were all settled, Mike volunteered to share his story first. He told about how his late wife Maria first developed cancer while she was pregnant with their second daughter, Keeva. Maria received three misdiagnoses prior. The doctors mistook the early stages of breast cancer for a clogged milk gland.

Keeva was only a week old when Maria was diagnosed. Mike and Maria focused their energy on her healing. They followed every recommendation and the first treatment worked, and Maria got better. But Mike remembered that she was never the same. In less than two years, the cancer had come back and had metastasized.

As he spoke, I started crying and I could not stop. The counselor got up and handed me the box of tissue that I desperately needed.

Mike continued sharing about his worries for the girls who wouldn't have their mother to help them through puberty and teach them what moms teach their daughters. He talked about how he had to cut their hair because he had trouble styling it. The more I listened, the more I cried.

Oh, Dios mio, how devastating, I remember thinking as the tears continued to fall. It also astonished me that this man took care of his late wife and young girls for the better part of three years. Ed's diagnosis, hospitalization, and passing was five months altogether and, at the end, I was exhausted and uncertain of how long I could keep my head above water.

I could only imagine the anguish and pain Maria felt when she knew she had to leave her husband with their two young girls. I was having such a hard time listening to Mike's story because I was thinking about my own story and seeing myself in Maria. She was a young mother and a teacher who loved her students. She gave everything to those around her. I thought of the little ones suddenly not having their mommy there to teach and guide them.

As all of these thoughts were swimming around in my brain, a clear voice broke through:

"You have it better, and here you are thinking about ways to give yourself leukemia just to prove where Ed's illness came from. There is nothing to prove and plenty of life to live."

Suddenly, I started repeating in my mind and as I continue to cry:

I am grateful for my life and for being here.
I am grateful for the time that I had Ed in my life.

For bonus material go to ...

I am grateful for my health and all my senses.
I am grateful for my two healthy and beautiful daughters.
I am grateful for my family.
I am grateful for Sharon.
I am grateful for Ruby.
I am grateful for my colleagues.
I am grateful for my job.
I am grateful for my friends.
I am grateful for Panchito.
I am grateful for my girls' school community.
I am grateful for my neighbors.
I am grateful for my apartment.
I am grateful that I am here celebrating Ed.
I am grateful for Alison's kindness. I am here because of her.
I am grateful for Healing Hearts.
I am not alone.
I am okay. I am okay. I am okay.

The more things I found to be grateful for, the better I felt. I stopped crying, and when it was my turn to share, I was able to do so easily. I felt calm and at peace.

I listened to every unique, yet familiar, story shared by the rest of the members of my group. We had all gone through the same feeling of losing a part of ourselves but still showing up in life because we care.

I felt so safe and loved in the support group. It felt like a warm blanket on a cold day.

Once the session was over, I felt so much lighter. I started walking toward where the kids were, and as I got closer, I saw Navah painting a friend's face and Kaya climbing a tree with Molly. The sun was shining bright and the breeze was gently caressing my face. I told Mike that I was sorry that Maria suffered for so long and that he had it worse than me. Mike told me, "One is not better or worse. Your husband was the picture of perfect health and, months later, he was gone."

Next up on the schedule for all of the families was a horseback ride. Mike offered to give us a ride and I gladly accepted. I sat in the passenger seat, and Molly, Kaya, and Navah were all in the back. As Mike adjusted their seat belts, Kaya said, "Mommy, Mr. Mike looks like Daddy but with hair."

I pretended that I did not hear it. My brain felt blank. I had no idea what to say, so I said nothing.

Months later, Mike would tell me that he felt like we were already a family during that ride.

The horseback experience through the woods was very beautiful and powerful. I saw patterns of leaves I had never seen before. I could hear the gentle water flowing in a nearby creek. I could see pretty butterflies fluttering. The sky was blue and bright. We were surrounded by beautiful wildflowers and scenery. I was beginning to feel recharged. For the first time in what felt like forever, I felt good.

Throughout the entire trip, I could feel Ed's energy and love.

For bonus material go to ...

Toward the end of the Healing Hearts retreat, we all gathered in a beautiful circle. The children were given a box with a butterfly that they released. Beautiful poems were recited, and each family shared a takeaway from the retreat. Also, the children were given the opportunity to say something that they remembered about their departed loved one.

Just before we left, Mike and I shared phone numbers to coordinate a playdate for the girls to see each other again.

Affirmation

Instead of writing out just one affirmation for this chapter, I invite you to write your gratitude list. Use it when the world feels hopeless, dark, and heavy. You can read it or speak it out loud. You can hang it on your wall. You can leave it in a place where you add to it each day. If you need help, I gave you a place to start and a healthy reminder to add to the end.

I am grateful for my life!

I am grateful for _____

I am grateful for _____

I am grateful for _____

I am grateful for _____

www.griefandgratitudebook.com

I am grateful for _____

I am grateful for _____

I am grateful for _____

I am grateful for _____

I am grateful for _____

I am grateful for_____

I am not alone.

I am okay…

If you feel called to, journal about what you are thinking and feeling as you write these out. Was it easy? Does it get easier over time? Sometimes it can be hard to feel grateful when it feels like the world has come crashing down around you, and you can't understand how something so tragic could happen to someone you love. I hear you. I have felt it.

Keep trying. Write about all the things you know you want to feel grateful for.

For bonus material go to ...

www.griefandgratitudebook.com

My Notes

For bonus material go to www.griefandgratitudebook.com

My Notes

Chapter 5

Healing & Growth

*"Life is not a problem to be solved,
but a reality to be experienced."*
– Soren Kierkegaard

5

I saw it happen. Two bereft people - a widow and widower who arrived after midnight on a chaotic trip to a bereavement camp. I saw them meet. And in that single moment, I saw a transformation from loss...to life...to love. This is a powerful story that brings me tears of joy each time I think of it. Have your box of tissues next to you as you read this. Be ready for the beauty and possibilities of life. Perfect.

-Claire Grainger-Valvano, LCSW

A few weeks after the Healing Hearts retreat, I received a message from Mike. He wanted to plan a playdate with the girls before I left for my solo retreat to Asia. Mike suggested that we meet for lunch before the playdate to have the opportunity to talk without interruption. We decided to meet for lunch in my neighborhood. I remember giving him a choice: Mambi restaurant, a traditional Dominican food restaurant; or Pick and Eat, a healthier eating restaurant. Mambi was Mike's choice. Great! I thought I would have a sancocho with white rice (a traditional Dominican soup with different kinds of meat and root vegetables).

For bonus material go to ...

On the day of our lunch date, I got a message saying, "Hi Jay, no rush, but I am in the area. I just wanted to let you know."

I felt a rush of excitement. It was great that we would be able to see each other and talk. He was such a caring, friendly, and sweet guy. I had just finished getting ready when he messaged me, so I walked to the restaurant.

There he was, waiting. I felt joy to see him again and thought, "Oh, he is taller than I thought!" Blue is my favorite color and, as I got closer, I noticed how blue and lovely his eyes were.

We shook hands and sat down. It was a very businesslike transaction. I'm smiling to myself as I write this now.

"It's so nice to see you again, Mike. Are you hungry?"

"I can eat!" he said with a smile.

With that, we both took a minute to decide what we wanted to eat and then placed our order. During our meal, I learned that Mike lived in New Jersey, and about 15 minutes away from Washington Heights, New York City, where I lived. Mike and I had so much to share about Ed and Maria that our lunch lasted about 3 hours.

"Do you think we should go?" I asked. "I feel like we should give the table back to the restaurant."

"Probably, but it's so nice talking to you."

"How about we wander to Le Cheile. It's an Irish restaurant that Ed and I have always enjoyed going to."

"I would love that."

It was raining when we got outside. I put my umbrella up and looked at Mike.

"Do you have an umbrella?"

"No, but I don't mind getting wet."

"Here. Don't get wet. There's lots of room."

"Great! Thank you."

As he entered under the umbrella, there was an unspoken feeling of comfort and peace between us.

Unfortunately, Le Cheile was closed that day. We crossed the street to another great spot, 181 Cabrini, and sat there for a drink. As we were waiting, we continued to talk about Ed and Maria. Out of nowhere, I just started crying. I couldn't stop myself, nor did I want to.

Mike put his hand on my hands and said, "I am so sorry you lost Ed; I know how much he meant to you."

My eyes met his and I said, "And I am so sorry you lost Maria."

For bonus material go to ...

We both paused for a moment and I moved my hands quickly.

"Can I tell you about something that I am so excited about?" I asked.

"Of course."

"I am taking a solo journey to Asia. I almost can't believe it. It's not something I ever thought I would have the courage to do. I am so afraid, but I'm doing it."

"Nancy, that is amazing. You are so brave for going on your own. Tell me more about it."

"Actually... you know what? I think we have to go. I have a medical appointment. And don't you have to get home for your girls?"

"I do!"

We said goodbye with a hug. It felt good to hug him.

As I sat waiting to be called into the room, I reflected back on my afternoon with Mike. I really enjoyed talking with him. He was such a good listener. I got to talk about Ed, and I did not feel rushed or ignored. All the comments he gave back were positive and empathetic. He understood that Ed meant so much to me and that my love for Ed will never end.

For a moment, I worried that I had talked too much about Ed. I quickly realized that if I did, I was not going to worry about it.

The worst thing that could happen was that after the girls had their first playdate, I was going away and that could be it.

That night, Mike called me.

"Jay, I hope you don't mind that I am calling. I had a great time at lunch. Can we meet again tomorrow? I want to share something with you."

"Sure. I only have about an hour though. Is that okay?"

He agreed and said, "We can meet at the other restaurant you had in mind."

"Great!" I hung up, wondering what Mike wanted to talk about. I was left to patiently wait until the next day.

Shortly after I entered Pick and Eat the next day, Mike arrived. He ordered smoothies for us, and we started to talk.

He said, "You can take this any way that you want, and I totally understand if you think this is crazy, but I have to put it out there. My palms are sweaty; I have butterflies in my stomach ... I have a crush on you! I understand if it is too soon. I am okay with that, but I wanted to let you know that you are occupying a lot of space in my mind. I felt these feelings yesterday, and it made me nervous and guilty. I was planning to cancel today. But I woke up this morning feeling depressed and tired, the same way I've felt since Maria got sick again. Yesterday was the first day in a long time that I felt good." (Mike would later tell me that he was singing when he was driving home over the George Washington Bridge the day before!)

For bonus material go to ...

I could not believe what I was hearing. I did not know what to say.

"Don't feel pressure; I will be here for you either way."

I thought this guy was amazing ... what a sweetheart.

I responded, "I am okay with that. I really enjoyed talking and spending time with you."

We said goodbye to each other. As soon as I got to my apartment, I rushed to tell Ruby all about it. I needed to talk to someone. Mike had started occupying space in my mind too, but I was going to continue with my plans for the solo retreat and the rest of the summer as planned.

I also called my cousin Yenie and I shared what had happened with Mike. "I think it's too soon," I told her. It had only been a few months since Ed passed.

Yenie just replied, "Jay, too soon? According to whom? Do not worry about others' opinions, for they have not walked your walk. Ed got sick and passed away within 5 months! We don't know how much time we have left. How do you feel when you are around Mike?"

"I feel great because I can talk about Ed, and he does not mind. He listens and knows what I am going through. And he can talk about Maria, and I know how he is feeling. I enjoy talking to him and it's comforting to share memories of a loved one with someone who understands because they themselves are going through it."

At that moment, I decided to follow how I was starting to feel. I embraced that I had met someone just like me, who was going through a similar journey, and with children as well. Sometimes it's normal to doubt; it's normal to feel that it's too soon. It's normal for you to feel like it's okay one minute and not the next. Do not do anything that feels uncomfortable or upsetting to you. If it feels good and just the thought of the other person brings you joy or hope or a smile to your face, by all means embrace it. You are worthy of feeling good.

Hold onto Life and Not Your Past!

At the end of June, Mike and I met with our girls at Bennett Park in my community. Kaya and Navah ran toward Mike, Molly, and Keeva. We were meeting Keeva for the first time.

Keeva, who was three, could not say Nancy, so she called me "Fancy." I felt happy to see Mike and his girls, and also to see our girls playing and having fun. Keeva was a cutie pie. She was so little and yet so fast that I could not take my eyes off her. We had breakfast at the park. While our girls played, Mike and I talked.

This playdate and meeting Keeva, who was only a few days old when her mommy, Maria, was diagnosed, helped me to understand that each moment in life is a time to live and hold. Seeing the four girls playing and happy to be together, alleviated

For bonus material go to ...

my pain. I actually enjoyed listening to the girls talk and laugh. It was so beautiful to see their glowing faces moving through the playground like fireflies on a summer night.

"God, thank you for this moment," I remember saying to myself.

When we were saying goodbye, the girls started to cry. Keeva was very upset and told Mike, "I want to stay with Fancy."

Mike quickly picked her up and said, "You will see Nancy again soon."

Keeva kept crying. As I walked back home with Kaya and Navah, all I could think about was Keeva. I did not like seeing her cry. It was a bittersweet moment.

Building new memories can be incredibly healing, and spending time with Mike's daughters and my two girls was definitely very rewarding.

Mike and I met for breakfast one last time before I left for Asia. He wished me well and gave me a beautiful card with some Thai currency in it as a gift.

"Mike, this is so thoughtful of you. Thank you so much for your generosity."

He responded, "I want you to treat yourself and have money available just in case you need it when you arrive in Thailand."

All I could think about was how he had to go to the bank ahead of time to do the currency exchange, and how very thoughtful it was of him to do that. It showed that he cared and that he was thinking of me. He had touched my soul, and I was filled with gratitude for his act of love and kindness.

Toward the end of our breakfast, I said, "I want you to take this time that I will be away to think about whether or not you want to date when I get back. I am 10 years older than you, and I want you to think about that."

"Your age doesn't matter; I like you very much and have not felt this way in a long time."

Mike was growing on me. I could not believe how caring, helpful, generous, and kind he was.

Finding Comfort in Your Own Movie

"You need to love yourself. Love yourself so much to the point that your energy and aura rejects anyone who doesn't know your worth."
– Billy Chapata

I got to JFK, checked in, and waited to board my flight. It was happening. I got a cup of coffee, sat down, and opened my journal. I started thinking about Ed and writing all the things that I was grateful for. I was writing and crying and crying and writing. I was also thinking about my daughters, whom Ed and I had never been apart from. Now Ed was gone, and their mommy was leaving for almost a month. I was dealing with so many emotions at that moment: fear, guilt, sadness, loss, loneliness, and worry, but also excitement and gratitude.

Once I was settled on the plane, I did a lot of thinking and writing. I replayed memories like a never-ending movie. My mind traveled back to August when we were having so much fun during our family vacation in the Dominican Republic. I thought about how happy Ed was, how happy we both were.

"Amore, we have something good going on! I love my family," he would say with a big smile.

I allowed my mind to replay the movie about the past. There were so many memories.

In September, after Ed shared that he would love to retire in the Dominican Republic, we began looking for a place to buy in Puerto Plata, but nothing materialized. It wasn't supposed to. I just did not know then that life had another plan for us.

October was when he started getting sick, developing infections out of the blue. Suddenly, he was tired and in pain.

In November, he was diagnosed and hospitalized. He spent his birthday, November 17, and Thanksgiving, at the hospital.

In December, he was able to come home from the hospital for three days for a visit. My cousin Antonio and his wife came to visit us, and I remember Ed being very nervous. He whispered in my ear, "Please, amore, ask them to wear gloves and put on masks."

January of 2019 arrived. A brand-new year was here. Ed's last visit to our home was on Martin Luther King Jr. Day. As a family, we spent the day teaching our girls about the life of Martin Luther King Jr. Being a biracial couple, Ed and I wanted to educate our girls on our country's history regarding issues of race and inequality. We also talked about how our country is a better place because of his contribution to the Civil Rights Movement in seeking equality for all. I remember that Ed got very emotional and said, "What a hero!"

The next day, Ed developed a high fever and had to return to the hospital. He felt safe at the bone marrow unit and less anxious. There was no intimacy. We did hug each other but that was about it. He hated being in the hospital away from his family but was also afraid for his health outside of the hospital. He was between a rock and a hard place.

February brought to us two perfect matches for Ed's transplant. As soon as Ed's health was stable, he would be able to undergo the procedure that could save his life.

Prior to the procedure, Ed needed one more chemo treatment. The doctor discussed the dosage with us. I remember asking him to please reduce the anticipated dosage. I was worried about the side effects and wanted him to be at his best before the bone marrow transplant. It was explained that a high dosage would be more effective since his last bone marrow test revealed a high percentage of cancer cells in the bone marrow. They thought this would better prepare him for the upcoming transplant. Ed got his last chemotherapy and, shortly after, he had a stroke that affected his left side and writing abilities. He lost his voice for about 20 minutes, and after this chemo, his stomach problems began.

For bonus material go to ...

"Ed, please drink the juice. It's an organic juice with berries, carrots, apples, and spinach."

He would take a sip or two and that was it. I remember getting upset that he was not eating. But again, I also realized that he could not. I felt disempowered and unable to do anything to help my husband. I had to surrender. It was not easy.

Ed was suffering. He was worried. He was detached and a bit cold toward everyone at the end. I remember that Scott, his childhood friend whom he loved as a brother, came to see him and spend some time with him. I shared with Scott that Ed was not talking much and was a bit distant. I asked him to please try to engage him in conversation and see if there was anything Ed wanted to share since he was going to spend the night at the hospital. Scott agreed.

When Scott came back to our apartment the next day the first questions I asked him was, "Did Ed share anything with you?"

"No, he didn't. He was not talking much." We both felt bad because we knew that postponing the transplant was very upsetting to Ed. He knew it was his greatest chance to heal and continue living.

A week before the transplant, Dr. Jercic met with us and explained that the transplant needed to be postponed. He stated that Ed's body was not ready as he continued to struggle with ongoing fevers and stomach discomfort.

Sitting on the plane, my mind went back to my last night with Ed. I could see everything. It replayed vividly in my mind again. I looked at my reflection in the plane's window. By this time, my eyes were red and swollen and I was feeling tired and sleepy...

Thailand

"The wound is the place where the light enters you."
– Rumi

It was evening when I arrived in the capital, Bangkok. As the taxi drove along unfamiliar streets, there was the most beautiful sunset. The ride to the hotel took about twenty minutes. I got out of the taxi, and the smell of delicious food hanging in the air reminded me that I hadn't eaten since I left New York.

I checked in, went to my room to drop off my bag, and went back out. I walked about 50 steps from the hotel to the restaurant where the delicious smell was coming from. I felt calm and grateful to have arrived safely. I enjoyed a noodle dish, a taro desert, and a cup of tea. The people were welcoming, friendly, and humble.

Having eaten, I was ready to continue planning the rest of my trip. Back at the front desk of the hotel, I was greeted and informed of the highlights of the area and the must-take sightseeing trips. I scheduled some trips, to the Golden Buddha, the temples, a floating market, and the Maeklong Railway Market. I also booked a boat tour that included treats and drinks. I was set!

For bonus material go to ...

The next day, I got up bright and early. At the front of the lobby, there was a driver waiting for the guests going on the Golden Buddha and Temples day tour. The bus was ready to go. Shortly after, we arrived at the elaborate temples. Everyone took off their shoes and started walking up the steps.

I looked at my feet, my toes, and took one step at a time. I wanted to live every second of the moment. To be present. To be mindful. It is such a sacred place. The breeze and the heat intertwined together. Everyone was quiet. I was alone. I knew no one and no one knew me... but we were all sharing the space, and our energy was magnified and powerful.

I was in front of the most beautiful thing I had ever seen: the Golden Buddha! I could feel the love through all of my being. God was within me. I knelt and started to pray. I stayed there for a long time. I allowed the sorrow and pain to be. I felt numb and lighter at the same time. I gave myself a big hug.

Once ready to go, I met my guide and continued to the Grand Palace and Buddhist temples. I learned the history and how many of these temples were built over one hundred years. The beauty was indescribable.

The next day, I booked an oil massage. They used a gentle technique that helped take the tension out of my muscles. I felt relaxed and my mind was calm. In that moment, I was so present that I actually felt every stroke, every touch. I focused on releasing the anger and the suffering. I was sending love and blessing thoughts to the two women using their hands and healing energy for my soul. I inhaled peace and acceptance, and I released suffering and anger. I focused on my breathing while I let the tears roll down the sides of my face.

These massages, I found to be infused with healing energy and love. In this time, you set yourself free and allow your body and soul to align. Your focus turns to the sweet present moment, and all of your senses are awakened.

I realized that the present was my gift, and this filled my heart with gratitude. I was grateful to be where I was. I was grateful to be able to feel and smell, and to be able to forgive myself for feeling guilty and for wanting to carry out a plan to prove where Ed's illness came from. I realized that I deserved to be here and that I was worthy of giving myself care and love.

You don't have to go to Thailand to enjoy aroma oil therapy or a hot stone massage. If you have not gotten a massage, I encourage you to try one.

Next on my list of places to see was the floating market, which was located on a river. I really enjoyed it. In Thailand, there are lots of local boats trading. These boats are filled with goods: tropical fruits, flowers, handmade crafts, ready-to-drink coconuts, and food that they prepare for you right on the spot. The food was delicious.

One of my favorite places was the Maeklong Railway Market, which is located on top of a railway line. The prices there were the best; and again, the food and pastries were amazing. I had a mango smoothie that was the most refreshing drink I have ever had.

For bonus material go to ...

It was busy there and, as I was walking, I saw a man killing live fish, and other things that you normally would not see in North America. Suddenly, I heard a sound and all the vendors pulled back their umbrellas. A couple of minutes later, the train passed just inches away from the shops and people. As soon as it passed, the vendors pulled their umbrellas again. It was quite an experience—unlike anything I had ever seen.

On this trip, I met a couple from Australia, who were celebrating their fiftieth wedding anniversary. We started talking, and when they asked me, "Are you married?" my eyes got watery.

"No, I am a widow," I responded.

"I am so sorry," the woman replied. "What happened?"

You know this part already, so I won't tell you again, but I did share part of my story with the couple before saying, "We were going to celebrate our ten-year anniversary this year."

"One of our friends just lost her husband to a heart attack. He was quite young as well. Not as young as your Ed, but still too young. She never had a chance to say goodbye. She is devastated."

It was my turn to feel sorry for someone else's loss. Their story was another reminder that I was not the only one going through a life-changing event. Sooner or later, we all have to deal with losing a loved one. All living things perish.

I dried my tears.

"I am happy for you both and send you so much love. What a blessing being married for fifty years to someone you love, care about, and can share everything with!"

Japan

Yes, Japan! Finally! I couldn't wait to meet Maki and experience Japan.

"How long are you here for?" the customs officer barked at me.

"Seven days," I responded.

She shot me a suspicious look and asked, "Why are you traveling alone?"

"Alone? Because I am choosing to go solo on this trip!"

Her glare got stronger and her tone more aggressive. "What are you planning to do here?"

"Well, I will be in Tokyo for a few days, and then I am meeting my friend, Maki, who will be my tour guide when we go to Kamikatsu."

"Kamikatsu?"

"It is a place I want to go to while I am here in Japan."

For bonus material go to ...

"Why there?"

Her angry expression made me nervous, but I managed to explain:

"I want to visit this region and learn more about Kamikatsu's zero-waste mission for 2020. I also want to experience the Japanese countryside and nature."

The questions finally ceased, and I was free to go. I took a taxi. I've never paid so much for a less than 20-minute ride! Taxis are so expensive in Japan that people hardly use them.

I got to my tiny room, and I was feeling miserable and upset. Being questioned about traveling alone was a trigger for me. I felt so vulnerable at that moment. The questions made me feel as if I was doing something wrong. Obviously, these questions were not very welcoming. And I was not going to share more of my story either.

This was a wake-up call. I learned not to assume. You never know what another person's circumstances are, or why they are choosing to do the things in the manner that they do them. In my case, I was traveling alone to release the pain and suffering and to take some time to detach from everything, as well as to provide my body and soul the time to accept my new reality. By doing so, I could allow myself to go through the transformation that I knew I needed.

In that tiny room in Japan, I let everything out. I went back and listened to every message Ed and I had exchanged using

WhatsApp. Ed had sent me the Paul McCartney song, "Silly Love Songs", about two weeks before his passing. But around this time, he was detached and not saying, "Amore, I love you," as much as he used to. He would say, "Amore, thank you for everything you are doing for me and our daughters," and "I could not have done this without you." I listened to the song over and over again until I could not cry anymore. I did not eat. I cried myself to sleep.

"I can't explain, the feeling's plain to me (I love you)
Now can't you see?
Ah, she gave me more, she gave it all to me (I love you)
Now can't you see?
What's wrong with that?
I need to know
'Cause here I go again

I love you
I love you

Love doesn't come in a minute
Sometimes it doesn't come at all
I only know that when I'm in it
It isn't silly, love isn't silly, love isn't silly at all, yeah, yeah

How can I tell you about my loved one?
How can I tell you about my loved one?
How can I tell you about my loved one? (I love you)"

– Paul McCartney, "Silly Love Songs"

For bonus material go to ...

Once again, listening to that song again and again, I lost track of the time. At one point, it hit me that I was thirsty, hungry, and tired. I could barely open my eyes; they were swollen and puffy, red and burning. I did not feel good.

Then a thought came to me: "No matter what happens, I am near and will always be with you; take care of yourself." It was so clear. I looked around and Ed was there too. I could feel his presence.

I responded out loud, "Thank you, amore. I love you."

I chose at that moment to end my suffering. I still felt a deep sharp pain in my heart, but I got myself up and took a shower, got ready, and went out. I purchased a few bottles of water, an egg sandwich, and a hot coffee before taking the train to explore Tokyo. Everything in this city was so clean and organized. The people were very helpful to me. And quite fashionable!

I found a place where I could have my makeup done and dress up like a Japanese princess in a kimono. So, I did. My makeup was done, and they took a while to put on the kimono. It was quite a process! At the end, I bought some of the photos and had some tea and treats. It was a great experience. The two ladies were sweet and kind. I shared my story with them, and I received two big hugs. I showed them pictures of my daughters. I felt the love of these two beautiful souls.

From here, I met Maki, and we took a small plane to Kamikatsu. Once there, Maki and I were picked up by one of the members of the zero-waste organization. They took us out to eat and, once again, the food was delicious. It was also healthy. The air in Kamikatsu was different; it was clean and clear. We were surrounded by many trees and there was a beautiful river.

We stayed at a place in town where a Japanese grandma would come and make our meals using fresh vegetables that she had picked in an organic garden. Maki and I also had the chance to pick our own vegetables from a community garden to make our own meals. We also visited a hot spring, which was quite a renewing and refreshing experience. I was a bit surprised and was blushing when I was told that the custom was to bathe nude. Stepping out of my comfort zone, I entered the spring the same way I came into this world! Although I felt uncomfortable at first, I felt a deep connection with the space. I was grateful for the beautiful experience I was having.

When we went to the zero-waste plant, I was amazed to learn how everyone worked together each day to have zero waste in the town. The recycling center had a place for everything. The seniors who could not drop off their recycling each week had a young person go to their house to collect it and bring it to the recycling center. Also, there was a room where people bought goods that they no longer used or needed and that others could have. I came back with two beautiful Japanese bowls!

The Waterfall in Kamikatsu

An eight-year-old on a bicycle came and told us that her grandma, the lady that was making our meals, had sent her to take us to the sacred waterfall. Maki and I followed the young girl as she took off on her bicycle. The waterfall was a fifteen-minute walk from where we were staying.

The cool air and the unique sound of the waterfall surrounded me. This was a highly spiritual place. Maki washed her hands and went up to pray. When she came down, I did the same.

I began my prayers by saying, "Gracias Dios por todo." Thank you, God, for everything! I then began identifying all the things I was grateful for. I felt at one with the space.

As my thoughts got quiet, a loud thought emerged: "Kai came to prepare you for Ed's passing. This was his role in this life experience."

I started to cry and thanked God once more for his love and compassion and for his kindness. I experienced the vivid manifestation of God in this sacred place. I then felt the urge to thank Ed and Maria. I knew without a doubt that it was them who had brought Mike and me and the girls together. We were meant to be together. Maria with the wig, and Ed via Alison, his social worker. I came down and Maki said, "Nancy, you were there for a long time! Are you okay?" I had lost track of time, but some of my questions were answered: I now understand Kai's role in preparing me for Ed's death and that Mike and I were meant to work as a team to move our girls forward in life.

Hong Kong

My trip ended in Hong Kong. It was a busy city and reminded me of Chinatown in NYC—not the easiest to navigate. There were lots of people, and the many intermingling street smells could get overwhelming. I had arranged to meet with a friend but by then decided that I did not want to spend time in Hong Kong. I missed my daughters, Pancho, my family, my friends, Mike, and his daughters. I had accomplished what I wanted to accomplish during my solo retreat. It was time to go home. I went to my room and arranged to end my stay there two days early.

Affirmation

Take a moment and write about one of your big dreams. Write about why it is a dream of yours and how you would feel if you could live that dream.

Why haven't you taken action toward making this dream a reality? Be honest with yourself. Is it because you are afraid? Is it because you do not feel you are worthy of happiness? Is it because you do not have confidence in yourself? See if you can figure out what is holding you back.

Once you've done this, with your big dream in mind, write out the following affirmations and feel each one in every cell of your body:

- I can achieve anything I put my energy into. Everything is possible!
- I am worthy.
- I am strong.
- I am confident.

For bonus material go to www.griefandgratitudebook.com

My Notes

Chapter 6

Happy Again

*"Count your age by friends, not years.
Count your life by smiles, not tears."*
– John Lennon

6

Days after I lost Ed, someone said to me, "When God takes something away, it will be returned to you the same or better."

I responded to this comment by saying nothing. I couldn't believe what I had just heard. I had just lost my husband, the father of my children, the man I had built a life with and one I loved with all my heart. I did not want to think about him being replaced. Of course, I wanted to be happy again in my life; I just couldn't see how that would be possible.

I have talked about how some of the things that were said to me after Ed's passing really got to me. I know many people had my best interest at heart, but sometimes I just did not want to hear what was being said. How did they know what I was feeling? How could they even begin to imagine the pain I was in?

I couldn't even imagine moving on at the time. My new reality was one I never imagined. The thing is that the person who made the comment about God sending me something the same or better, didn't get it exactly right, but the words weren't necessarily wrong either. I did encounter new opportunities—not the same or better, but different. These new opportunities brought happiness and abundance into my life.

For bonus material go to ...

The Power of a Dream

A month before Ed's passing, I had a dream that I was older, walking on a beach, with soft waves caressing my feet. It was warm with a cool breeze. I was holding hands with my husband. I was happy and in love and feeling so content and at peace. As I looked up at my husband, the man that was holding my hand, I saw a tall, strong, handsome man with a head full of hair.

I woke up puzzled. I had not felt this way in such a long time. It was all a dream. But I was in love; I was holding my husband's hand! But that husband was not Ed. Ed was bald! My mind searched for the man in my dream, and I realized I didn't know who he was. Then I felt guilty for having such a beautiful dream, even though the dream did not make sense. I did not want it to make sense. All I wanted was for Ed to get better and come home to his family. I wanted our lives to go back to normal.

Looking back, this dream was a sign that despite the pain and anguish that surrounded me, I was going to be happy and in love again. Pay attention to the signs, dreams, and conversations you have with other souls. They carry messages that can pave the road we are about to walk.

I remember talking to a parent, Ahna, who I met at the girl's school because Kaya and her twins were in the same kindergarten class. Many times we met at dismissal and walked down to a nearby park and watched our children play. One day while our kids were playing, Ahna shared the story of her sister who had passed from Acute Myeloid Leukemia a few years earlier. Ahna told me about her treatment and that she had been a donor match.

Her sister did not survive. Little did I know at that time, about two months later, Ed was going to be diagnosed with leukemia as well. Ahna's story indirectly prepared me because, when Ed got diagnosed, I was familiar with some of the information. Reflecting on the conversation with Ahna made me realize that we are all linked and often don't even realize it.

Written in the Stars

Two families becoming one was written in the stars! The way Mike and I met was as if our meeting was coordinated by a higher power or our destiny. I haven't shared this yet, but I did intentionally try to avoid Mike and Molly at the retreat. No matter how much I talked to Kaya and Navah about staying away from Mr. Mike, it did not matter. Every time they saw Mike and Molly, they would run to them like I had not talked to them at all. It was frustrating and embarrassing.

Finally, I gave in, and before saying our goodbyes, we talked about setting that first playdate, where we would meet Keeva for the first time. When we did meet for that first playdate, I felt a deep connection with her, and Keeva also quickly became very attached to me. I felt maternal love for her instantly. Having lost her mommy at such a young age, I felt that she was part of my life and that we belonged together.

At this point, I knew in my heart that I was feeling love for Mike and that if he was around when I came back from my trip to Asia, he was going to be the one. I had decided that I wanted to be with someone going through the same thing I was. And he was so easy to talk to. I was very attracted to him, not only for his looks but for his big, caring, and compassionate heart. He was always very respectful, and I liked that.

Navah's Need for a Stepdaddy

I really enjoyed our playdates and spending time not only with my daughters but with Mike, Molly, and Keeva as well. During our time together, I usually followed Keeva around because she was as fast as lightning and only 3 years old. I was nervous about her getting hurt. Then I learned that Navah would ask Mike during our playdates, when I was not around, if he could be her stepdaddy. I had no idea she was doing this until I learned about it much later. It was a secret between Mike and Navah. Apparently, I was not supposed to know. After Ed's passing Navah had expressed that she wanted more time with her Daddy and asked me for a "New Daddy". She enjoyed it when Ed would pick her up and place her on his shoulders. She had so much fun going out when it was just her and Daddy. The two of them had their own unique rituals and games that she missed. I knew that she wanted a father figure in her life. She learned that Daddies are fun, loving and caring. At the retreat, she witnessed how fun Mike was when he would play with Molly, Kaya and her.

Keeva's Need for a Mommy

Almost every time we ended a playdate, Keeva would cry and at times have tantrums. She would say, "I want to stay with Fancy."

Mike would have to pick her up because she would not walk. It made me feel so sad every time. I felt an incredible connection to Keeva. I was worried about her and Molly. Then, one night, Mike and I were talking over the phone, and I asked about the girls.

"Keeva keeps talking about you!" he replied and gently laughed.

What can Keeva be saying? I thought.

When I asked, he responded, "You don't want to know."

"Of course, I do! What is she saying?"

"She wants you to be her mommy."

"Well, tell Keeva that I will always be here and that she can come any time!"

That day, I knew I wanted to be part of Keeva's life. I knew that her Mommy was diagnosed a week after she was born and then had to battle cancer. I knew that Keeva did not remember much about her Mommy because she was so little. I felt immense love for her, Mike, and Molly.

Painful Memories and Healing Connections

Molly was five and had vivid memories of her mommy, Maria. Molly was hurting, and when she shared a memory of her mommy

For bonus material go to ...

falling while going to the bathroom, I knew how worried and scared she had been. Her daddy had left her and Keeva with a neighbor. I was all ears, and at the end when she was done sharing, I asked her, "Can I give you a hug?"

She opened her arms and, with tears in her eyes, held me tight. I felt her pain, anguish, and feelings of hopelessness. These feelings, I embraced with a heart filled with love and compassion. I whispered, "I love you, and I am here for you. I am so sorry your mommy had to leave you and your daddy, and Keeva. Sometimes these things happen, and we don't always know why. One thing I know for sure is that you are a brave little girl who will always have her mommy close to her heart. Thank you for sharing."

Shortly after that, Molly and Kaya were wearing "Maria and Ed" T-shirts while making a memorial for them and sharing memories, crying, hugging, and connecting emotionally. They were healing and building new experiences as a result of accepting and connecting with their grief. Being that Kaya was my first and Molly was Mike's, they developed a strong bond quickly.

The Joy of the Present Moment

When I returned from my solo retreat, I felt overwhelmingly happy. I was experiencing each and every moment as it came. I could not stop hugging and kissing my daughters. I gave my mom and Ruby a big hug and thanked them for taking care of the girls while I was away. There is no better feeling than being at home. Shortly after my return, Mike and I met up, and it was one of my happiest moments in a long time. I shared my experience and we talked about our feelings and the desire to date each other.

Ocean City

Mike had planned a long weekend vacation for us. At this point, we wanted to know what would happen once the six of us were together for more than a playdate. This was a very wise decision. We had a wonderful time. The girls got along beautifully, and we discovered that we were the perfect team! Mike and I continued to share memories of Ed and Maria. The girls shared memories about their parents in heaven. It was a memorable weekend.

We all went to the beach and, shortly after we got there, Kaya said, "Mommy, Daddy and Maria in heaven brought us together. They are so happy. I will make a picture of what I am seeing in my mind."

Goosebumps covered my body in that moment. Going into this weekend, Mike and I had felt it would determine our future together as a family. Mike and I were thinking not just about us but also about our girls. They had been through so much, and we did not want to start an emotional relationship that was not going to support them in their grief and healing. Not only did they lose a parent, but Kaya and Navah had also lost Uncle Joe, Ed's only uncle on his father's side, whom they loved and were very attached to. Molly and Keeva had lost their maternal grandparents, Bernie and Luke, who were not only their loving grandparents, but neighbors down the street who were deeply involved in their daily lives, less than two years before Maria had passed. Sadly, they both also lost their battles with cancer and died only six days apart. Our goal was to protect our daughters from any more emotional pain and turmoil.

Our daughters would talk about Mike giving me an engagement ring. They would cut flowers, give them to me, and say they were from Mike. The truth was that our daughters loved being together, playing and taking walks. They were so happy, and their happiness filled our hearts with joy.

The more time Mike and I spent together, the more our love grew. We got along so well that it was hard to believe. We helped each other out with the girls and learned quickly that two adults with four kids was easier than one adult with two. Even though we had more kids together, it was easier with a partner.

Iceland

One day, Mike asked me if I would like to go with him to Iceland.

"Only if you promise to keep me warm!"

"I will keep you warm anywhere!"

A few weeks before Mike and I were talking about traveling, I had mentioned to him that I wanted to see the Northern Lights.

My friend, Samantha, had visited Iceland and told me how much she loved it.

Also, we wanted to go to a new place that neither one of us had been before. We both wanted to talk about our future together and have the time away from the girls to just be and connect.

And so off to Iceland we went. Again, traveling can be very stressful for some couples, but for us, it was easy sailing. While there, we talked a lot. It was here that we decided we both knew that we wanted to formalize our relationship.

The Engagement Ring

When Mike proposed, I was not expecting it. He caught me by surprise. I knew we both intended to make our relationship official, but I didn't know when Mike was planning on proposing. Behind the scenes, Mike had reached out to Mark and Elba. Elba called me and asked if I could meet with her because she had a few things to share. She was a bit overwhelmed by her older son, Maddox, turning 10! I agreed to meet with her at Pick and Eat for a late lunch/early dinner. It was at Pick and Eat restaurant where Mike had shared, months earlier, that he had a crush on me. As our meeting date was approaching, she texted me and said that her husband Mark wanted to join us and that it may be a good idea to also invite Mike. I agreed, but again, thought nothing of it. I told Mike that my meeting with Elba now included Mark, and I asked if he would join us. He agreed.

For bonus material go to ...

The date came and we left for NYC to meet with Elba and Mark at Pick and Eat. My friend Katherine had been looking to spend some time with the girls, so I arranged for her to stay with them for the evening.

Mike and I arrived at Pick and Eat, and Mark and Elba were not there. I texted Elba and did not receive a response.

"This is unlike her," I told Mike. "Let's just wait a bit longer."

"Well, let's go upstairs and wait there. Let's get something while we wait. What would you like?"

"A fruit smoothie," I replied.

I went upstairs and, shortly after, he joined me.

"I have not heard from Elba. This is so strange."

He reached into his jacket pocket, got down on one knee, and said, "Jay, will you marry me?"

I could not believe what was happening. It felt like another dream. At this point, I knew that Mike was the husband in my dream!

I got emotional. We hugged and hugged and kissed and kissed.

"You, Elba, and Mark fooled me!"

"They are waiting for us at Guadalupe," he replied. Guadalupe is a Mexican restaurant in Inwood, NYC. Once there, we celebrated love, friendship, and life, with some delicious appetizers and drinks. I remember feeling overwhelmed with joy and looking forward to sharing the news with our daughters, who I knew could not wait for this moment to happen.

My engagement ring is so beautiful and special. It has seven diamonds: a center stone symbolizing Mike and me as one, and then three stones on each side, representing Ed, Kaya, and Navah on one side, and the other side representing Maria, Molly, and Keeva.

Then I learned of all the planning and coordination Mike did to make our engagement one of a kind. For example, he called my mom, who was out of the country, to share his intentions and ask for her blessing. He then took a trip to Long Island to visit my father and stepmom to ask for their blessings as well. This warmed my heart. It showed just how much he loves me!

When we shared the news with the girls that we were engaged, they jumped up and down with excitement.

The Extended Quarantine

COVID-19 arrived and the cases in NYC were increasing rapidly. Mike expressed his concerns and asked me if I would consider staying in his house with the girls. He was worried about us getting sick, and also concerned that a quarantine might prevent all of us from seeing one another. Also, in Mike's house in New Jersey, the girls would have a backyard and more space to

For bonus material go to ...

play than in their New York City apartment. I agreed to stay over for the quarantine.

During this time, we really bonded. We grew to love each other even more. It was a time to continue going through the healing of our grief, a time to be kind and enjoy our girls, and a time to be grateful that we were alive.

Our girls were so excited about the wedding that they helped me with the assembling of the invitations and setting up the favors. They patiently waited for the big day.

Two Weddings, One Big LOVE

Mike and I ended up marrying twice. We had a civil and then a church wedding. At our first civil wedding, we had a beautiful memorial for Ed and Maria, with their favorite treats and photos of each family. We also had specific music played to remember them, as well as a moment of silence. This was a wonderful celebration after months of the pandemic and being locked up in our homes. It felt good to be outdoors and celebrate love, family, friends, and those who will forever be in our hearts.

Our second wedding was at our local church. It was very small and intimate. A month after our second wedding Keeva, asked me "Mommy, will you and Daddy get married a third time? I want to have fun and dress fancy again!"

Love is Kind

Mike and I have a special bond. We both come from something greater than ourselves. Part of our journey is to move our daughters forward in this life. We owe it to the girls, Ed and Maria, and us. Our friendship and relationship keep strengthening and deepening. We are consciously very kind and gentle with each other. We are both thankful to be here and grateful to have met.

Cherish the Love and Keep the Passion Alive

When I knew that Mike was the one, I decided to share my feelings with him and communicated them with a louder voice, expressing my feelings to him as they surfaced. "Mi amor, I freakin' love you!"

Mike responded, "Mi reina, I freakin' love you too!"

Or I would say, "Tesoro mio, you make me so happy. You make my soul sing."

I remember telling him, "Mi amor, even if I had placed an order to have you made, you wouldn't be as perfect as you are! You're perfect for me." He always responds with something sweet, loving, or kind.

Why do we do this? Because we feel so much love in our hearts, and we don't want to hold back. Holding back from openly talking about the way you feel, will prevent you from letting those you love know how much they mean to you.

"When you know better, you do better," said Maya Angelou. This quote has always resonated with me. Here I am, feeling in love and having another opportunity to love another soul with my mind, soul, and body.

For me, intimacy has become a sacred act where two souls become one, experiencing each other with all of their senses. This is pure magic, and having the opportunity to do so with someone you love deeply and care about is an indescribable feeling.

I decided that I was going to love Mike without reservations and be fully present at all times, especially during intimacy. This decision has transformed our lives. What is one thing that I want to do with love for my husband, to show how special he is in my life? I love coconut oil, and I use it on my face and my body all the time. So, every night after intimacy, when we are feeling relaxed, happy, and a bit sleepy, it's my time to continue enjoying myself by giving Mike a face, neck, and chest massage. I enjoy giving him love this way and cherishing our time together in a very special way.

If you don't have a partner, you can always give yourself a face massage. Show yourself love. Remind yourself how wonderful, beautiful, and creative you are.

Life's Blessings

"Live your truth. Express your love. Share your enthusiasm. Take action toward your dreams. Walk your talk. Dance and sing to your music. Embrace your blessings. Make today worth remembering."
– Steve Maraboli

It was definitely a blessing having Mike in my life. It was an adjustment at first because, as a sole parent, you get used to doing things your way. I remember, at first, Mike and I would talk about everything. We would talk about the girls, their needs, activities, as well as the things that I was doing and needed to do. A relationship without communication is like a plant without water.

I even remember the first time that he was going to take care of the four girls for a few hours, and saying, "Are you sure you can handle the four girls for a few hours?"

"Well, of course! You don't trust me?"

I instantly worried that he might be offended.

"Of course, I trust you! It's just that four may be a lot! Please call me if you need me."

He did not call, but that afternoon, shortly after I came home, he said, "I know now what you meant earlier about the girls. Oh boy, oh boy!"

If you have young children filled with energy and strong wills, you know what I mean. They can be a handful. We made sure that we were on the same page without taking anything personally or making assumptions about what the other person was thinking. We were there for each other and aware of our daughters' needs and acted accordingly.

A New Family, a New Dynamic

When people ask me about the dynamic of my new blended family, I openly share that like any family, it's challenging at times but filled with many happy moments. It's an adjustment and, when new situations arise, you just have to go step by step. You learn and you tweak things a bit.

Mike and I talk about expectations and meet with our girls regularly. This way, we listen to them, and they listen to us, and then we can come up with joint solutions. The key is developing an understanding that everyone needs to be on board with. Everyone has to agree to do their part while showing mutual respect, working as a team, and enjoying our time together.

Acting From the Heart, Not From the Ego

I am very mindful of thinking before speaking. I try to ask myself: "Is what I am about to say coming from love and my heart or from my ego?" This is a great way to keep yourself in check. You may say something a certain way, but it's unknown how the other person will take it. As long as I feel good and I act from a place of love, I don't worry. I know that eventually the right outcome will take place. This is why important conversations are best in person, not via a text or email.

The best advice I can give you while going through your grief and also having a relationship is to be open-minded, communicate clearly, be flexible, and always remember to be kind with your words. Take turns speaking. If you don't have something nice or positive to say, then don't say it. Always approach a difficult topic or situation without blaming or making the other person feel guilty or shameful. These are low frequency feelings, and they don't uplift anyone.

You can say things like, "I don't quite understand what you mean." Or, "I need to take some time to reflect on that. It was not my intention to hurt your feelings." Or, "I am sorry if I hurt you." Or, "Okay ... I did not think of it that way."

Take the time to express your needs and place yourself in the other person's shoes. It does not have to be "I" or "you" all of the time. Sometimes it can be "us" or "we." Give yourself the opportunity to be who you are and embrace what you bring to the union.

Responsible Parenting Is Not Always Easy

As responsible parents, we came to the conclusion that we needed to have the conversation again about who would care for our daughters should anything happen to us. Mark and Elba, Kaya's godparents, had originally agreed to take care of Kaya and

For bonus material go to ...

Navah if anything happened to Ed and me. Mike and I decided that we didn't want our girls separated if anything happens to us. We knew that it was in our best interest to have all legal matters in order. This would avoid unnecessary stress in the event that anything should happen to both of us.

Be aware that going through grief also means the reorganization of your physical space sooner or later, as well as taking care of legal matters, especially if you have young children. I remember that this conversation, when Ed and I first had it, was very emotional for both of us. I was angry and upset and came home crying that evening. You may experience similar feelings. And it's all normal because the mere thought that you could die and leave your children can be indescribable. It was a conversation that forced Ed and me to face that cruel side of reality.

At the moment when Mike and I had to have the same conversation, I was going through it for the second time, not with two but four daughters. Mike and I updated our wills and spoke to Mark and Elba about a topic that was familiar to us. We made the call. Elba answered the call and without hesitation said, "Yes! Of course, we would take care of your girls!"

I remember tears running down my face because I realized how full their hearts were with love and compassion to agree to such a huge responsibility.

Our New Family and Our New Home

Today, Mike and I, together with our daughters, continue celebrating Ed and Maria. We often say, "There is no us without them." We are two families who were joined together as one by grief, healing, and love. We have a special bond and have so much love for each other. Our daughters love each other and get along better than I ever remember getting along with my siblings. Mike and I realize that this is because of their unique bond.

We bought a big house because, with four girls who are growing, having more space is helpful. Ironically, we have empty bedrooms every night as our four girls continue to sleep together in the same room, just as they have done every night since we all moved in together during COVID-19. Every night before bed, we pray together, "Dear God, please watch over Maria and Ed. Maria and Ed, please watch over us." The girls continue to be inseparable and look out for each other, especially at school. They love playing and spending time together.

In our new house, we created a garden with a plaque and a tree in Ed and Maria's memory. This way, we have a reminder of their unconditional love and kindness.

God's Plan Is Perfect

Mike and I met at a perfect time for us! Our daughters continue to bond, and our love continues to grow. I am so grateful every day, and it is with this grateful heart that I wish the same for you. Your journey will be different. Your healing will be

For bonus material go to ...

different. But always remember that you are worthy! You are worthy of love. You are worthy of joy. You are worthy of achieving your goals.

God will give you what you need. Something has been taken away, but something wonderful is on its way. The one thing you need to do is open your heart, soul, and mind.

Affirmation

Help yourself open your heart to receive love, your life to new opportunities, and allow your soul to find alignment in your new path. The following affirmation is simply a suggestion, so if it does not resonate with you, please write one that does.

Your openness affirmation is:

I am willing to receive all of the abundance in every area of my life. The Universe is here for me. It is waiting for me to accept its gifts.

_____
_____
_____
_____
_____

www.griefandgratitudebook.com

My Notes

For bonus material go to www.griefandgratitudebook.com

My Notes

Chapter 7

Children & Grieving

"Grief is like the ocean; it comes in waves, ebbing and flowing. Sometimes the water is calm, and sometimes it is overwhelming. All we can do is learn to swim."
– Vicki Harrison

7

"Mommy, it was not fair that Daddy never came back from the hospital! I wanted more time with my daddy!! Mommy, can I have a new daddy?" screamed Navah.

I knew exactly how she felt. I wanted more time with her daddy too. There is a wave of sadness and anger that washes over when you want something so badly and you know it will never be. How do you help a child handle this emotion, when you barely know how to handle it yourself? It broke my heart that she and Kaya had to know grief at such a young age.

I had to explain to Navah that there was no such thing as a new daddy.

"Stepdaddy is what you will call him, Navah; but Mommy is not ready for that, and a stepdaddy will never replace your daddy."

I held her hands and looked into her tear-filled eyes. "The good thing is that you have so many memories of your daddy that you can go back to."

Then I walked her to where we kept our photos. I brought out a set of photos from when she was a baby. She paused on the one of her daddy holding her for the first time, and the one of the whole family together.

For bonus material go to ...

"How do you feel when you look at these photos?"

"I still feel mad." She paused for a moment... "I think they make me feel a little better."

I took comfort in looking at the photos of our happier days together, and I could tell that even though Navah wasn't completely sure, she did too. At this moment, I went with my gut as a mom. You will do this, too; but remember to stop, try to be present, and simply listen.

At this time, Navah was 5 and Kaya was 7. Navah's response to losing her daddy was to get angry. She wanted another daddy to play with, learn from, and go on outings with.

One of the special things Ed always did was give each daughter time alone with just him. He would take turns taking each one out. He felt that spending quality time with each daughter individually was important. These moments allowed him to bond with his girls and create special memories with each. I know they both looked forward to these moments and truly missed them.

Just like you, your children will experience a range of emotions in each stage of their grieving process.

At one point, I remember Navah asking me, "Mami, what are my friends going to say now that I don't have a daddy?"

"Navah, you know that each family is special and unique. You have friends with one mommy, two mommies, a mommy and a daddy. Also, do you remember Timothy in your class?

"I do."

"Well, he lost his mommy and now he just has a daddy. Sometimes families lose a daddy, a mommy, a grandpa or grandma, or an auntie or uncle."

She grabbed me and said, "Mommy, I don't want to lose you!" and started crying.

I responded, "Navah that is why, when I talk to God, I always ask for a long life. I want to be here for a long time so that I can hold you in my arms the way I am now."

Kaya's response to losing her daddy was different from Navah's. She cried often. She often wanted to talk about Ed, which I loved doing. It was and still is important for me to keep his memory alive with the girls.

Kaya also needed a lot of comforting. She wanted to be held and often asked to be picked up.

"Mommy, do you remember that Daddy used to take me to school every day?"

"Of course, I remember."

"I miss Daddy, Mami."

"Me too," I replied with tears, and crouched down to give her a big, long hug.

For bonus material go to ...

One night, I heard some noises coming out of the girls' room. As I walked closer to the door, I heard Kaya saying, "Daddy, I miss you so much. I love you, Daddy. Why did you leave, Daddy? Take me with you!"

When I heard her say "Take me with you," I opened the door. I was shocked and saddened by what she had said. The second she saw me, she got very upset and said, "You are not supposed to listen when I talk to Daddy!"

I got nervous. I knew I had responded irrationally by barging into her room, but I was so upset by hearing her say she wanted to go too. I slowly walked over to her and sat beside her.

"I am so sorry, sweetheart. I know that you are upset. I am upset, too, that your daddy is no longer with us in physical form. Kayita, Mami loves you."

My words calmed her. She hugged me, and as we held each other, we both were crying. Shortly after, she was asleep.

No mom wants to see their child hurting. I had this need to make their pain go away, and I think that one of the most difficult things was knowing that I couldn't. I could walk beside them. I could do my best to make it easier. But Ed was gone, and there was nothing I could do to bring him back, other than to keep his memory alive. I knew that Kaya needed support and I continued to find therapeutic opportunities to help her through her own grief.

Listen, Learn, and Love

"What we once enjoyed and deeply loved, we can never lose, for all that we love deeply becomes part of us."
– Helen Keller

I have learned so much about myself as a mom since Ed died. I am stronger than I ever thought possible. I have so much capacity for growth. While my new normal as a single working mom of two young girls, who had just lost her husband and the father to her children, was terrifying at first. However, I realized that it was something that I had to accept. Here's the thing: You can either accept it or not, but life will be much easier if you come to this realization sooner rather than later.

I had to step up. There was no question. I had to build a life for myself and my girls that saw us swimming rather than drowning. It was important to me that they thrive in our new normal. To do this, I had to be present and listen. I had to continuously be open to learning new skills. And most of all, I had to love. My goal was to surround Navah and Kaya with love.

Of course, I made mistakes. I am human. But I always tried to learn from them, to be my best and to do my best, for my girls and for myself. I know you are hurting. I know it's hard. But your kids need you, and I know that you, too, are doing the very best you can.

For the rest of this chapter, I want to share with you some important lessons I have learned along the way. And as always, take what resonates with you and ignore what does not. Grief is experienced differently by everyone, including children.

Be Emotionally Available for Your Children

One of the most important lessons I have learned is that children have their own needs and unique ways of dealing with the loss of a loved one, as you saw in the stories I just shared.

Also, depending on their age, they may feel more or less comfortable speaking about their departed parent or loved one. This can be a bit challenging at times because you, as the remaining parent, are also working through your grief. You are dealing with your own emotions and pain. You also have more responsibilities as the sole parent. And on top of all of this, you need to be present for your children.

They need your love and your patience now more than ever. No matter how I was feeling, I would drop everything and get closer to whomever was having a hard time that day. Your child needs to know that they are your priority and that how they feel matters. You, as a parent, need to reassure them that the way they are feeling is part of the grieving process that they are going through. Sometimes it was Kaya, and other times it was Navah. Sometimes I would find both of them crying. Sometimes it was me who needed a hug and wanted to hold them close.

www.griefandgratitudebook.com

Talk to Your Children, Be Transparent

The more information your children know, the better. When they are informed, they will have less questions. Don't try to hide the severity of a parent's illness from your child, or it will hurt both you and them in the long run.

I talked with Kaya and Navah about Ed's illness right away. I explained what acute myeloid leukemia was. We talked about the treatment their daddy needed. We talked about how he wasn't getting better and that he was suffering.

I told them that we had nothing to do with Daddy's illness. It just happened and we did everything we could. The nurses and the doctors did their very best, but Daddy did not get better. These things sometimes happen, and we don't always have an answer as to why they happen, but they do.

Losing a loved one can have a major impact on anyone, especially children. It can also be confusing depending on the age of the child, who may think that their loved one is coming back. When losing a parent after a separation or divorce, there is a possibility that the parent can come back and/or that the child will see the parent again. However, the grief after the death of a loved one carries a very profound message: *I am not going to see this person again.* This can be extremely painful for a child or anyone.

After losing Ed, someone said to me, "The less you talk about the death of Ed in front of the girls, the faster they will forget."

For bonus material go to ...

I responded by saying, "That is showing a lack of transparency, and I don't want my daughters to ever forget about their father."

The idea that the children would do better and heal faster, or forget, if the adults around them stopped talking or sharing memories about their departed loved one, is not a healthy way to help your child cope with the loss.

A way to be transparent is to connect emotionally to the pain, anger, and sadness your child is feeling. Together, feel these big emotions. This takes time and practice, but the more you connect and talk about the thoughts that come into your mind and share your feelings, the better your children will feel. This will empower them to also share their feelings with you.

We cried together a lot. We wore his t-shirts often. When feeling cold, we would each wear one of his favorite sweaters. Kaya loved wearing his hats. The more we talked about Daddy, the less pain and sadness we felt.

Shortly after Ed's passing, Ahna walked up to me at dismissal. She then shared that she had a beautiful dream about Ed. In the dream, Ed was outside sitting on a table. He told her that he was doing well. I was nearby and she called me so that I could see that Ed was okay. I got closer but I was not able to see him. She told me that, in the dream, Ed was holding a baby in his arms. Then she said she woke up.

This gave me goosebumps as I had not shared with Ahna about the loss of Kai. I thanked her with tears of joy, for this was Ed's way of communicating with me to let me know he was with Kai. I gave her a big hug.

The girls knew that they had their older brother, Kai, in heaven, although they had never met him. They saw two photos of him that came in a very special aqua blue box, which was given to us when we left the hospital after his loss. I shared Ahna's dream with them, and I reminded them that Kai was not alone anymore because Daddy was with him. This was powerful.

Love and Reassurance

Sharing your feelings with your children empowers them to do the same with you. This encourages them to talk about their feelings and to be physically and emotionally available. They need to feel connected to the parent that they lost and to you as well.

You can help them to integrate their grief into their lives. Share your dreams, memories, and thoughts with your children. When a situation arises, tell your child what their loved one would say or do in the situation. Share their phrases. Talking and sharing about their personality brings them alive and closer to you and your children.

Provide your child with lots of affection. It is important that they understand that you are emotionally connected with them. They need to feel like you are with them. Tell them how much you love them and how they are helping you during this time as well.

Reassure them that they will be cared for and that you are there for them no matter what.

For bonus material go to ...

Listening Is the Key

Invite your children to talk to you about what they are feeling. It is important not to force your children into a conversation and to let them know that it's okay if they choose not to engage in one. Go with the flow. Some children need a bit more time than others to share a memory, a wish, or a story.

Listen to what they say. Be present. Push everything else aside and make listening to them your number one priority. This is part of their healing. When children are sharing their feelings, thoughts, hopes, and dreams, and having their questions answered, it helps them cope with the loss and integrate the grief into their new life.

Don't ask too many questions, and don't interrupt them when they are speaking. The more they share, the better. And this can be hard at times and will require patience. The more they tell their stories or share their memories, the easier it gets and the better they will feel.

Provide Normalcy and Consistency for Your Children

A healthy grieving process comes from normalcy and consistency. Children need to continue with their regular lives as much as possible. Going to school, to the playground, and engaging in activities that they enjoy is extremely important.

Consistency promotes stability in unstable times. I kept the same routines that the girls had when Ed was around. They still go to bed at 7:30 p.m. I still take them to the park every Saturday morning. We still follow the same rituals when visiting Ed's mother, Sharon, in Connecticut.

Sometimes, we will go to Uncle Joe's favorite restaurant, the Manor Inn in Connecticut, for a nice meal. Uncle Joe was Ed's father's only brother. He was also Ed's godfather. Uncle Joe took us there many times when he was alive. Ed was very close to him, and I loved him as I would a grandpa. He loved Kaya and Navah and would wait for us with treats for the girls every time he knew that we were going to visit him. The girls loved him and enjoyed playing with him. When Uncle Joe passed, it hit us all hard. Both Kaya and Navah knew that once someone dies, you don't see them again.

Creating New Rituals

Integrating your grief and accepting the loss of your loved one helps in the healing process. For us, creating new rituals to celebrate and remember Ed, was extremely important. For example, after his passing and since it had become just the three of us, during dinner time, we started listening to Daddy's favorite music and sharing a memory. The girls and I would talk about how Daddy was not with us physically, but he was with us in spirit. We chose to honor him each time we sat down for dinner.

For bonus material go to ...

We also have an annual mass for Ed around the time of his anniversary. After the mass, we go out to a restaurant to eat with friends and family, recalling and sharing memories of him.

Every November, we celebrate the day of the dead. On this day, we eat Daddy Ed's and Mommy Maria's favorite foods and treats. Again, we share memories and/or look at photos.

We often go to Ed's favorite restaurant, Refried Beans, in Washington Heights. I will often eat the vegetarian burrito, his favorite!

We posted a mandala that we created at Healing Hearts Retreat, with colors and words that reminded us of Daddy.

We visit Daddy's grave anytime we want and bring flowers, painted rocks, and small trees. Ed's favorite flower was the daffodil. He thought that this was the most beautiful flower every time we would see it in early spring. He loved their bright yellow color! When we visit the cemetery, we often leave daffodils to decorate his memorial.

We donated Ed's surfboard to his surfing instructor in the Dominican Republic. Now, other people who love, or even want to try, surfing can use it in his memory. We gave some of Ed's belongings, including some of his cherished guitars, to friends and loved ones. We kept anything that had sentimental value to us. Kaya kept many of his T-shirts, and I did too.

We kept some of Ed's guitars and play them often.

We watch the YouTube videos he uploaded from our wedding.

We talk about how wonderful it was to have had Daddy Ed in our lives, and about all the love he gave us, the care and the support, and the fun times we had together. It's important to show love and gratitude for the good times your deceased loved one shared with the children. One rule I believe should be followed with children is that you don't say anything about a departed one that you would not like someone saying about you when you are no longer in physical form.

Here are some ways to celebrate the departed loved ones with your children:

- Share a memory together at dinner time.
- Create a memory box for your children to add notes to their loved one.
- Watch Ed's videos interacting and playing with the girls.
- Watch old family movies together.
- Look at photos together and talk about the moment they were taken.
- Make a memorial and have a family photo of you and your children and their departed parent.

Creating new rituals was a great vehicle to help us go through grieving and healing.

For bonus material go to ...

What are some of the ways that you are or would like to celebrate your loved ones?

_____
_____
_____
_____
_____
_____

Get Professional Help

Attending the Healing Hearts Bereavement Retreat was very helpful for the girls. This provided them with the opportunity to meet other children going through the same experience, make new friends, and create new memories. They were engaged in indoor and outdoor play and did special activities that reminded them of their daddy or mommy. Furthermore, this provided our girls with a safe space to share memories about their daddy and mommy in heaven.

I enrolled Kaya and Navah in art therapy, and this helped them tremendously. They were able to talk about their daddy and share stories, play music, and make drawings for and about their daddy.

I remember that Molly would go weekly to see a counselor at CancerCare because she had a hard time talking about her mommy, Maria, with anyone that was not Kaya and Navah. This helped her greatly; Molly would share old memories about her mommy and talk about new memories that she was making with us.

Counseling and therapy can also help if your child is experiencing any of the following:

- Withdrawal
- Difficulty speaking
- Feeling guilty
- Physical symptoms, like headaches or stomach pain
- Loneliness
- Not wanting to leave the house
- Self-destructive behavior

Counseling provides the opportunity to talk and share feelings that are not so easy to express with the parent or caretaker. Some children may feel that if they openly share their feelings, their surviving parent will get upset or sad, so they refrain from doing it. This was the case with Molly. Mike would often try to have conversations with her and she would always answer, "I don't want to talk about it." She would only open up to Kaya and Navah and would tell them, "I don't want to talk about Maria with Daddy, because it will make him sad." Mike felt fortunate to have the girls as a support for Molly as well as the wonderful staff at CancerCare. Give your child the opportunity to be able to speak freely with someone with whom they do not have to worry about how they will react.

For bonus material go to ...

Playdates

Give your children as many opportunities as you can to have fun and enjoy life. Mike and I arranged for a lot of playdates with our girls. We noticed that during this time, the girls were happy. They talked freely about Ed and Maria. If they got emotional and cried, we would see them hugging and comforting each other. They looked out for one another, and they did not want to say goodbye.

Navah also enjoyed spending time with a classmate who had lost his mommy to cancer. After a playdate, she came home talking about how the daddy was taking care of the four boys and that it may be too much for him now that his wife was in heaven.

Children develop sympathy and understanding when they are given the opportunity to relate to others going through the same experience that they are.

Affirmation

One of the main points I want you to remember is that children are resilient and they adapt quickly to new situations. Yes, they need your love, care, and support to help guide them through their grief, but they are strong. And you are doing an amazing job!

www.griefandgratitudebook.com

Write this:

My children and I are strong together. I am doing the best I can with what I know now. I will keep learning. I will keep growing.

_____
_____
_____
_____
_____
_____
_____
_____
_____
_____

For bonus material go to www.griefandgratitudebook.com

My Notes

Chapter 8
Make the Shift From Pain to Power

"Don't let pain define you; let it refine you."
– Tim Fargo

8

In this chapter, I want to share with you some of the lessons I have learned through my own grieving process, first with losing Kai and next with losing Ed.

Why am I coming back to this in a later chapter?

Well, I believe that it's important for you to know that when you lose a loved one, there is a back and forth. Memories have a way of sneaking up on you when you least expect it. This is normal. It is a part of the deep hurting you are feeling. However, this is also part of your healing.

Allow Yourself to Grieve

These are some of the things you are probably experiencing now, and that you will continue to experience in the future but to a lesser degree:

- A lingering feeling of general suffering
- A deep pain that moves to different parts of your body
- An inability to stay in control of your emotions
- A debilitating fear for the future
- Moving from one task to another without a sense of direction
- An overwhelming sadness that you can't move away from

For bonus material go to ...

- A desire to revisit the moment when your loved one departed this Earth before your eyes, again and again and again

Dealing with these experiences does get easier. You can feel the wave of sadness before you completely succumb to it. You learn how to navigate: how to manage and when to release and just feel. When you feel a moment like this coming on, take a deep breath. Find a quiet place anywhere you are and ask yourself, "What do I want to go back to? What specific moment?" Sort it out in your mind and GO BACK to that memory and allow it to move through your experience one more time.

See your loved one in your mind; see their face, hair, head, hands, or body, and any details you want. See the person looking back at you with immense love and appreciation for being there. Feel their heart energy, filled with gratitude for all you were able to do for them when they needed you the most.

Feel the love ... there's so much love there. Tell them anything you want, and release any memory of guilt, anger, and resentment; just release it and see these big emotions leaving your body. Remember to breathe in and out. Do this until you feel calmer. Don't rush. You can do this more than once at different times. In a way, it is a meditation. When you are done, treat yourself to something that you enjoy, like a meal or favorite drink.

www.griefandgratitudebook.com

Release and Heal

"Stay focused on your purpose, not your pain."
– Ranal Currie

When you connect to a past experience that is overwhelming, it does not feel good going back to it, so know that you have the power to change it. See it the way you wish it would have happened, releasing any negative thoughts and feelings that may have been trapped inside your body for a long time.

Give yourself permission to release it and allow your healing to take place; go through the experience. Acknowledge where you are at the moment. Feel the pain, cry, and let it out again. Keep doing this. This memory may come back again in the same way. Keep releasing. Sometimes you will want to fight. It's hard to feel these things. It hurts like a deep wound that keeps getting reopened. Allow the wound to open; keep working at cleaning it until it is healed. The wound will still be there, but the pain will diminish.

When you are ready, make your way to the kitchen, pour a glass of water, hear the water filling your glass, and say:

"I am grateful for this healing water that will refresh, calm, and bring peace to my being, for now I have released (name the feeling) _____ toward (name of your departed loved one) _____."

For bonus material go to ...

For example:

"I am grateful for this healing water that will refresh, calm, and bring peace to my being, for now I have released the *anger* toward *Ed for promising we would grow old together*.

Feel what you're saying. Really feel it. Say it again. Feel it even more.

Then take your time drinking the water. Hear yourself drinking it. Visualize the water refreshing every cell in your body, bringing peace and a sense of calm. You may have to drink two glasses, one after the other.

Once you are done drinking the water, bring your hands to your heart and say:

"I am well.
I am feeling well.
Thank you."

And as you are saying, *I am well*, feel that you are indeed okay. Feel what that means to you, in your body. Do you feel lighter? Do you feel more energized? Do you feel inspired?

Give yourself a big hug. Show yourself love and gratitude. Each step brings you closer to healing and accepting your grief.

I have used this strategy many times and, each time, I feel better. Sometimes, after completing this exercise, I take a shower, get dressed, and start the day over again.

This may work for you if you try it. Moving through your grief at your own speed is what matters. Believe that you can do this, and you will. You have the innate ability to deal with adversity in your life. Remember, these strategies have worked for me. It may be beneficial to seek professional help, as having a face-to-face meeting can be a more powerful intervention, as well as provide you with comfort.

Take the Scenic Route, Not the Shortcut

"Grief only exists where love lived first."
– Franchesca Cox

When you are grieving, you do not want to cut yourself short. If you do not allow yourself to grieve, you will hold all of the emotions within yourself and this may hinder the healing process. You have to grieve, even if you no longer love the person you lost. Feelings and emotions are complicated!

Whether you did or didn't love a person who is no longer part of your physical space, bed, and no longer sharing the household responsibility, memories will come to your mind, from the good and not so good experiences you once shared, especially if there were children. You will have stories to tell.

I once met a widow who was thrilled that her husband had passed. She said, "I can finally live my life after 35 years of misery." She had two children with her husband of 35 years. However, she shared that she had stopped loving her husband a long time ago but stayed in the relationship because of their children. I was unable to relate to her, having been so devastated by the loss of Ed.

However, every loss brings an opportunity for self-assessment and life reflection. Reflecting on your situation, circumstances, and your life brings learning, and now you can go ahead and reach for what your heart desires. This is powerful and it can happen both ways: losing someone you loved with all your heart, or losing someone you did not have these strong feelings for.

Stop Hiding From Your Grief

When you hide from your grief, the sadness, the pain, and the feeling of sorrow is trapping your grief. Believe it or not, consciously or unconsciously, when you do not allow yourself to go through the grieving process, it can cause you harm.

How? Well, your health can be impacted, and illnesses can develop.

What can you do? I would recommend finding a way to release these big emotions that have been trapped within your being. Let them out by crying, screaming, hitting a pillow, or by doing anything that comes to mind that will allow you to let go and experience your feelings, without compromising your safety and those around you. You can also talk to a parent, a sibling, or a friend, or seek professional help. It's critical that you connect and identify where in your body you feel the pain. Describe the pain (sharp, comes and goes, etc.) and send healing thoughts and love to that area.

The bottom line: Feel and deal with your grief to enhance your healing.

Do Not Let Yourself Become a Prisoner of Your Grief

Set yourself free by channeling your grief. What does channeling your grief mean? It's another way of unleashing those big emotions and connecting with the pain that is now rooted deep inside the cells in your body.

Release these emotions that have been hurting you for a long time. It's one of the healthy ways to liberate and sustain yourself going forward. By doing this, you make peace and accept the pain that the loss has left within you. Channel this new energy by setting your intentions for what it is that you wish to create in your life.

Do you want to create illness, or do you want to feel good, blessed, and healthy?

Shift your energy and focus on yourself and your purpose in life. Try to connect with something that brings you fulfillment and bring it into your life. For me, I am able to find this feeling of satisfaction going out with my camera and taking photos of nature.

For bonus material go to ...

Embrace Your Good Thoughts and Feelings

Perhaps just like it happened to me, you may be thinking or saying to yourself, "I want things to feel good. I want my life to be better. I want to feel joy in my life. I want to be happy. I want more energy or more focus. I want clarity in my life, and it would be great to clean and declutter..."

In this situation, consciously focusing your attention on the present moment may help you reorganize and rethink of ways to start living your new life. This is all part of the grieving and healing process. When you are mindful, you're thinking about the decisions that you are making and have an understanding of why you are making them.

Old Sayings, New Realities

"Everything that has a beginning has an ending. Make your peace with that and all will be well."
– Jack Kornfield

You probably have heard these phrases:

The past is gone.
The future is not promised.
All you have is the delicious present moment.

Well, these common phrases became very present in my new reality as I started exploring and integrating my grief into my life. My grief is part of the person I've become. Kai was gone; I never held him alive in my arms. Ed was gone too. I could no longer hold him or hear his laugh. Even though those moments are now part of my past, they are a vivid part of my existence, for the love I feel has not changed.

Think about it this way: Now you have to hold two things in your heart—the love you still feel and the pain of their physical absence. Your goal is to integrate both to create your new reality and a balanced life where new experiences are welcome and seen for what they are: an opportunity to be you and seek happiness.

The things that Ed used to do that made me laugh, I think of them and they make me smile, and I can also think of the things that he would do that "got under my crater." He was sarcastic and I did not like it. I would snap at him and say, "Mi madre, Ed, otra vez!" (My mother, Ed, again!) And he would laugh and respond, "Okay, amore, give me a break." The good thing about Ed was that he listened to me when I was upset, and he worked hard to change the behavior that upset me.

I also loved that Ed and I had conversations about our own personal development. We'd talk about habits that we wanted to break. We supported and were honest with one another.

Is There Anything That You Would Like to Change or Develop?

Become aware of what you would like to change, refine, develop, or accomplish in your life that resonates with you. For me, it was meditating and being connected to the present moment. I also wanted to be open and non-judgmental toward others. I wanted to accept people just the way they are. I also felt the need to spend more time alone in self-reflection.

Some of your goals might be to eat healthier, travel more, or spend more time with loved ones. Try writing out both daily and weekly goals. When I did something, I crossed it out and found that it gave me a sense of accomplishment. As this happened, I began to write more goals. I found that this exercise helped to keep me more focused and motivated. When you intentionally write your goals or your heart's desires, these actions guide your thinking and you will be able to start attracting these gifts into your life.

Revisit the Past Without Leaving the Present

In many ways, I have begun to see my grief as my ally. Having your grief as your ally is beneficial because you will find that feeling good becomes easier and easier, and that you are able to sustain feelings of joy, happiness, and excitement for longer periods of time.

To clarify what I mean by this, here is an example:

Recently, I saw a beautiful clouded sulphur, a medium-sized yellow butterfly. I immediately thought of Ed, and a memory came to me from one of my visits to the cemetery shortly after his burial. I acknowledged the memory and the feeling and quickly said, "Hi Ed, I miss you. Thank you for visiting me today."

I continued to admire the beauty of the butterfly as it fluttered around me for a few seconds. Then it was gone, and so was my thought of visiting Ed's grave. I did not feel sad; I felt at peace. You may start noticing moments like this, where the memory comes to you without the pain, allowing you to sustain it and appreciate it in a gentle and loving way.

Balancing Your Grief

During my grieving process, I had to balance the parts that inspired and brought joy to my heart, and also accept the ones that upset or hurt me. In my case, not having Ed in bed with me, the loss of our intimacy, missing our deep conversations at night, and not celebrating joyful moments with our daughters together was painful.

Also, Ed would coordinate with our babysitter, Lorraine, one Saturday evening a month, for just the two of us to go on monthly dates. These were happy, cheerful, and passionate times for us. We enjoyed the time together to celebrate our relationship, love, and life.

I realized that Ed's energy was always around and that it was important to continue to go out; he was not there physically but was still spiritually present.

I then started to go out with Kaya and Navah for "Mommy and Me" dates. I also arranged dates with my friends. For me, it was important to keep Ed's memories alive by continuing to do the fun things that we did together. Sometimes, I will have a drink that he likes: "Ed, here is a Guinness to celebrate you and the love that I have for you!"

With these choices, I am creating a balance and, at the same time, finding a way to celebrate Ed.

How Can You Bring Balance into Your Life?

Think about this question and see what comes to your mind. Which areas of your life do you feel need less/more attention? Are you staying at home 90% of the time and going out only when you have to? Are you waking up and feeling grateful for the brand-new day, or does every day feel the same? At the end of the day, are you undressing to change into your pajamas, or have you stayed in them all day? Are you able to find gratitude for some of the good, or does everything feel bad?

If you are staying in, what are some ways you can entice yourself to get out?

If you are unable to get out of your pajamas, it may be time to seek professional help.

Sometimes it is the help of others that can help you find more balance.

www.griefandgratitudebook.com

What Does Creating Balance Mean to You?

A simple way to start creating a balanced life is by going through the grieving process by continuing to do activities that you used to do with your loved one. This is a way to keep their memory alive and create new ones. These new memories will start to bring the balance needed to allow you to start experience joy and happy moments again. This aids the alignment of your personality with your soul. When you do this, it also helps you minimize the development of unhealthy habits. Habits can be hard to change once established. If you are not mindful of them, they can become part of the new you.

Post-Traumatic Stress Disorder (PTSD)

PTSD, by definition, is an anxiety disorder that develops in reaction to physical injury or severe mental or emotional distress, and we know that losing a loved one is a traumatic event. I have talked to many widows and widowers and realized that just like grief, we all cope with traumatic events differently.

Many people begin to feel better over time, and some have sought professional help and therapy. The focus of the therapy is to help the individual overcome the trauma when the person learns the way they think and feel about the trauma.

The following are some of the therapy treatment options available to you or anyone suffering from PTSD:

For bonus material go to ...

- Cognitive processing therapy (CPT). This is a type of cognitive behavioral therapy. The patient undergoes a 12-session psychotherapy program that teaches ways to evaluate and change the upsetting thoughts. And we know that we can change the way we feel by changing our thoughts.

- Prolonged exposure (PE). This is another form of psychotherapy, where a safe and supportive environment is provided to help the patient work through painful memories.

- Eye movement desensitization and reprocessing (EMDR). This form of therapy has eight steps, where the patient is asked to recall traumatic images while the therapist creates a sensory input.

These are all treatments that are available and reported to have great outcomes in helping the person get back to living again.

Please keep in mind that when dealing with the grief of a traumatic event, self-destructive behavior can impact your health, your life, and that of those around you. Things to watch out for, during grief or after a traumatic event, are:

- *The use of too much alcohol,* at home or in outings, as a way to escape.
- *The use of illegal drugs,* as a way to forget and not feel the pain.
- *Having sex with multiple partners, without intimacy,* to feel love.
- *Irritability,* for anything and everything, and not knowing why you are feeling irritable.

- *Isolation*—no desire to see or interact with others around you, to avoid feeling the pain.

These vices will distance you from your true purpose in life.

The beauty of it all is that you can reflect, connect, and make changes to your behavior and environment to create ways to grieve without putting yourself at risk. You can learn ways to control your emotions and not allow your emotions to control you. Understanding why you are feeling an emotion or what is triggering it helps you find ways to feel better or to give yourself a break. Acknowledging any feelings of pain and understanding their origin, can support a healthier grieving process. By doing this, you will avoid developing new and unhealthy habits that are not in alignment with who you really are and the things that make your heart sing in life.

Positive Vibes

Maintaining a positive attitude that is aligned with happy thoughts and good feelings will bring you more opportunities to sustain that state of being. It is the same when feeling sad, lonely, and in despair.

One of the things that helps me stay positive is to recognize when a thought pattern is going to pull me back to the past, the suffering, and the anguish, and then I thank it and release it. I then start thinking about how full of gratitude and love my heart is. I am thankful that I am alive and connected to life and others around me.

For bonus material go to ...

Be polite and respectful to everyone you encounter. Try to smile more. You will notice that smiling creates an instant connection with those around you. Greeting others and being friendly is another way to maintain an elevated state of being and happiness.

Notice those around you and give compliments when warranted. I enjoy telling others "You have a glow... are you in love?" This will often make us laugh and enjoy our interaction! Purchase flowers or a plant for someone you love. Consider getting fresh flowers for yourself and place them in your bedroom or in a place where you will see them often. This will brighten your day!

Is Not Luck but Rather a Positive Attitude that Makes All the Difference

When you experience adversity, learn to appreciate the little things that make life so enjoyable.

I lost count of how many people tell me: "You're so lucky!" Usually, the person that tells me this has not given birth to a stillborn baby and had the experience of coming home without the pregnancy nor the baby, and having to start all over again. They have not had a miscarriage early in a pregnancy. They have not lost a partner to an illness unexpectedly. They have not experienced sexual abuse by a paternal grandfather, a loved one who was supposed to protect and guide them.

www.griefandgratitudebook.com

I wouldn't consider myself lucky, but I do consider myself a strong, positive person who is not a victim. I have effectively dealt with these challenging situations and created a balance in my life, because I am worthy and because my life is my gift. This is exactly why I learned not to assume. When I speak with someone, I know that I don't know that person's journey in this life. I don't know what the person had to do to overcome adversity. Many, if not all people, have had or will have one or more traumatic event in their lives.

As individuals, we deal with adversity differently. This is okay! These experiences are meant to bring learning and understanding into our lives. I believe that each instance of adversity is an opportunities to learn, grow and become a better person. In turn, this will support the evolution of my soul and expand my consciousness.

So, it's not about luck. It's about your attitude toward your experiences. Even if you are going through something devastating, there has to be something in that experience that gave you comfort, or something that you were grateful for. Perhaps you had an encounter with somebody who was kind. Once you find the moment, hold onto it. Feel good and relish it a bit longer to recognize the feelings of joy. Learn to consciously release any thoughts that no longer serve you.

For bonus material go to ...

The Magic of Intention Setting

**"Live with intention.
Walk to the edge.
Listen hard.
Practice wellness.
Play with abandon.
Laugh.
Choose with no regret.
Appreciate your friends.
Continue to learn.
Do what you love.
Live as if this is all there is."
– Mary Anne Radmacher**

I want to share with you a simple, yet powerful exercise that I learned from Ester Hicks, an inspirational speaker. Every morning before I get out of bed, I set my intentions. I started doing this more consistently and consciously shortly after losing Ed. It helped me to set it as one of my daily goals.

I visualize and state verbally or mentally what I want to see happen that day. For example, I take the George Washington Bridge to go to work. Those of you who have taken this bridge know it can be a nightmare.

On the days I go to work, one of the things that I say when I wake up is: "Easy sailing from home to work and from work to home or anywhere I drive today. I will only attract polite and caring drivers just like I am." And I smile.

I also think about the people I will be interacting with—my students, colleagues, parents, etc.—and I see myself having rewarding, positive, loving, and caring conversations.

I also give thanks for the new day, my family, friends, and everything that brings joy to my heart. This way, I don't let the energy of others influence the outcome of my new day, my gift, and my present. Additionally, every morning, I find at least five to ten things that I am grateful for. I do this continuously throughout the day every day.

At some point in the day, intentionally and with a grateful heart, I give someone a compliment or thank them for something that they did that "filled my bucket."

Ways to Live Your Life Intentionally

I invite you to think about your routines and decide what you would like to see happen in your day, each day. Set your intention upon rising and notice the subtle changes that you'll start to experience as the day unfolds. Use this page to journal about this after a week of giving it a try.

If this exercise resonates with you, keep doing it until it becomes part of your everyday routine, and you will see and experience a lot of magical moments in your life.

For bonus material go to www.griefandgratitudebook.com

My Notes

Chapter 9
Thoughts Become Things

"Change your thinking. Change your life! Your thoughts create your reality. Practice positive thinking. Act the way you want to be, and soon you will be the way you act."
– Les Brown

9

I find the quote on the previous page to be very true and powerful.

Ed once told me, "If you don't think you can do it, you won't be able to. If you think you can, you will. It's up to you. Your mind will follow your command. It does not care if it's good or bad."

We all have the power to choose a positive thought over a negative one.

Our words have a lot of power and so does our thinking when combined with our feelings. Our thoughts and actions are constantly paving the roads we encounter. As previously mentioned, during my grieving process there was a point when I was entertaining negative and unhealthy thoughts.

We have many conversations. Sometimes, with others. Sometimes, with ourselves. Believe it or not, you talk to yourself more than anyone else. Sometimes, these talks may become toxic. You will attract what you focus on. Some of these conversations will cause you to disconnect and isolate yourself from the world around you. Illness can come in the form of both physical and mental. Negative self-talk can become a habit and part of your personality. This may create negativity in your life.

For bonus material go to ...

When you start feeling a certain way that is a product of your thoughts, whether you are experiencing positive or negative thoughts, they tend to manifest in your reality. They become part of your experiences. If you are wondering why a certain situation keeps happening, the answer may be in observing your thoughts. I had to become very aware of my thoughts, feelings and thinking patterns.

Have you ever thought of a friend or a family member and within minutes or days you get a text or message or bump into the person that you were thinking about?

Filled with excitement, I said to a colleague during our lunch break, "This is great! I confirmed that our thoughts manifest into our reality...they become things!"

She responded, "See this is your wishful thinking again!" I don't believe this. It's being naïve to think that way." This is another example, to illustrate that whatever you believe in is your reality. I understand that my thoughts and the way I feel emit high or low frequencies that are matched in the physical form. I will choose to continue with my wishful thinking. It's great!

The works of Masaru Emoto, a Japanese researcher and author who wrote the book, *The Message from Water*. The finding of his work fascinates me because he was able to show that the human consciousness could affect the molecular structure of water. So, if our thinking and words and intentions can affect and change water molecules, imagine what it can do to our bodies.

Play with this concept and see if it resonates with you. Or you may be just like I am: reaping the benefits of consciously entertaining your positive thoughts and feelings and holding on to those as much as possible to attract what you want into your life.

> "What the other person says or does cannot really annoy or irritate you except you permit him to disturb you. The only way he can annoy you is through your own thought. For example, if you get angry, you have to go through four stages in your mind: You begin to think about what he said. You decide to get angry and generate an emotion of rage. Then, you decide to act. Perhaps, you talk back and react in kind. You see that the thought, emotion, reaction, and action all take place in your mind. When you become emotionally mature, you do not respond negatively to the criticism and resentment of others."
> – Joseph Murphy

Embrace Your Grief and Transform Your Negative Thoughts into Positive Ones

Embracing your grief is to experience and accept your pain and anguish in that moment. Feel it with every cell in your body. It may be that you're feeling sad and discouraged or lonely… or experiencing a marathon of feelings and can't identify the one that hurts the most. Don't be afraid to embrace these emotions and cry

For bonus material go to ...

if you need to. Send your breath with love and gentleness to that area that hurts the most once you have identified it.

You may be having many ongoing thoughts, running one after the other, again and again. When this happens, say aloud to yourself: "The way I feel is normal!" Acknowledge the thoughts. Instead of holding on to negative ones, thank them for confirming the pain from the past and quickly release them.

When you consciously release the thought, see or imagine it as a bubble fading and disappearing. Then take action. For example, if I was crying, I would get up, rinse my face, make myself a cup of hot coffee, and read a magazine or a book. Or I would write all the things I could think of that I was grateful for. This exercise would immediately raise my energy and I would feel better.

Sometimes I would get ready and go out. I would mindfully focus on my feet moving, the sounds of the birds around me, my breath, and the things I was seeing. Just being outside and focusing on what I was doing, and allowing myself to feel the moment, was uplifting and energizing. And then I would start having positive thoughts, such as:

- "Life is beautiful; it's nice and warm."
- "This is a great day to be here and now. It's wonderful that I can walk independently."
- "Being alive is a gift that I have and cherish."

I would hold onto these thoughts and feelings for as long as I could. Every time I did this, I felt open and ready to fully enjoy the experience and honor it.

I encourage you to try these strategies and see what happens. If you practice this, you will notice that you may start feeling better by letting the moment be, and by noticing all the beauty around you and by accepting that you're worthy of feeling good.

Mindfulness

Many of you may be familiar with the term "mindfulness," which refers to a mental state achieved by focusing your awareness on the present moment. While living in the present, you calmly acknowledge and accept your feelings, thoughts, and bodily sensations. This can often be used as a therapeutic technique to help you in your grieving process.

Prior to Ed's passing, I was familiar with this term. However, I did not integrate the act of mindfulness into my life until he was gone. I remember multitasking while doing something; I was always thinking about the next thing that I needed to do. It was challenging for me to just be and focus on the task at hand. In my mind, I did not want to waste time, and wanted to get things over and done with. The sooner, the better!

What I did not realize was that I was not fully enjoying the small and beautiful moments that these experiences were carrying with them. Once I noticed this, I realized that it was all in my conditioning. I recognized that the practice of mindfulness does not have to be time-consuming. I began to understand that it improved my awareness in everyday life. I also began to enjoy life's little moments more fully.

For bonus material go to ...

At first, it is necessary to put in some conscious effort to make mindfulness part of your daily routine. This effort and consistency breaks your old conditioning and retrains and shifts your brain into developing new habits. This process is called neuroplasticity. Neuroplasticity is the brain's ability to change and restructure itself. Studies have shown that mindfulness impacts the regions of the brain associated with stress, memory, empathy, and sense of self.

"Eventually, your cognitive skills will wane, and thinking and memory will be more challenging, so you need to build up your reserve," says Dr. John N. Morris, Director of Social and Health Policy Research at the Harvard-affiliated Institute for Aging Research. "Embracing a new activity that also forces you to think and learn, requires ongoing practice and can be one of the best ways to keep the brain healthy."

The most important thing to remember as you begin mindful practice is to be kind to yourself. It takes patience, time, and dedication to develop a new skill and habit, especially one that can have such a major impact on your daily life.

After making a conscious choice to be more mindful of the present moment, I had to keep reminding myself to "be here now," or "be mindful."

In many ways, I was having a conversation with myself. Something like:

- "Okay, Nancy, this is happening. How are you feeling about it?"

- "I think I am okay."
- "I see! How does it feel to be okay?"
- "Light. I feel light in my body. I feel like I've got this."
- "Amazing! What is your next step?"
- "I need a moment to figure that out, so that I don't get anxious, stressed, or overwhelmed."
- "I like the feeling of calm, serene..."

With time and with practice, being mindful becomes part of what you do. It becomes second nature. You will continuously begin having these inner dialogues with yourself. When you notice you are out of the moment, stuck in the past, or are worried about the future, you will have the ability to gently refocus to the present.

How do I do this, especially on the tough days when the negative feels like it is going to completely overwhelm me?

I go back to feeling, sensing, and being in the environment that surrounds me. A few ways to do this is by using your senses and asking yourself the following:

- What do I see in front of me? (Literally, describe to yourself the physical place. Is it a wall in your bedroom or a crowd at the mall?)
- What colors do I see?
- What do I enjoy about what I see? What pulls me back into the negative thoughts?
- Is there something that is bothering me in my space? Is there something triggering? If so, can I remove myself for a moment to take a breath?

- What does the physical space feel like? Is it warm or cold? Is there a breeze?
- What are the sounds that I hear? A television on in the background? People? Birds?
- What am I wearing? Does it make me feel good? (If not, and you are able to, go change into something that does.)
- Can I smell anything? (I usually carry mint and lavender oils with me. Later on, I will give you a bit more information about essential oils and their benefits.)
- What am I feeling emotionally? Is there someone with me who has triggered me? Can I talk to them about how I'm feeling, or ask them if I can take a moment to be on my own?

If none of this works, take a moment and just breathe. Focus on your inhale and your exhale. Do it again and again and again. When you are ready, come back to noticing what is around you in the physical world. Just the act of focusing on your breathing can relax you and ease the thoughts you are having.

Being mindful helped me when I realized that I was falling back into suffering. It helped me then and it helps me now. Mindfulness has improved so many areas of my life: in my relationships, at home, at work, and everywhere I go and with everyone I encounter. Additionally, there is a vast amount of research that shows that mindfulness can also improve your overall physical and mental health as well as symptoms of PTSD, anxiety, and depression.

I have learned that facing each experience I was encountering, with an open mind and a grateful heart and with kindness, helps me in making decisions with ease. Think about it; your mind is constantly thinking. There are so many decisions to be made at work, at home, and even during times of leisure. Sometimes those decisions are unconscious, or you may not give them your full attention, even when making an important decision. This can cause unnecessary stress and anxiety. It's important to remember not to rush through anything.

Take each moment as it comes and experience it—all of it! This is life. It is yours to experience! Your life is important!

Connect and experience the moment. This can be hard at first but creating that awareness and connecting to the experience is powerful. I remember telling myself, "What is the rush? I am here now. Let me actually listen and tune into the person's emotions." I call this listening with all of your senses and beyond. When you catch yourself moving quickly from one experience to the next without listening or engaging, notice it and mindfully redirect your attention to the precious moment and start over again.

The Practice of Mindfulness Is Like a Growing Seed

Have you ever planted a seed or garden?

I love gardening. Before Ed came home the last time before his passing, I followed his doctors' advice and got rid of almost all of my houseplants, as they could have potentially released mold into the air and caused an infection. I chose a home for each of my plants because I wanted to give them to people who, like me, would love and take care of them. After Ed's passing, I went to a

For bonus material go to ...

garden center and bought seeds and plants to replenish and surround myself with their beauty. I found gardening to be therapeutic, relaxing, and fulfilling. I enjoy watering them and learning what each one needs. Some need more sunlight and some need less. It is the same with water.

After Ed's passing, I noticed that I was talking to my plants more and kissing their leaves. I realized that I had started mindfully caring for my plants and, at the same time, learning about who I am. I love the seedling process the most. At this time, you can see the baby plant beginning to grow. There is magic here! You can actually see it peeking out and greeting you. At this stage, the small plant is vulnerable yet filled with life and beauty. The next phase is to patiently wait. You know, with time, it will become what it was meant to be: a beautiful plant, flower, or tree. This is similar to the way you may look at yourself in the process of starting over again.

Feeling worthy of a new beginning can be a result of any life circumstance or traumatic event you may have experienced.

I invite you to try seeing yourself as the tiny plant that you are caring for, by watering, providing it with nutrients, cleaning it, and giving it love and affection and the space to grow and develop. Not only are you the tiny plant, but you are also the gardener of your own life. This is a powerful metaphor. By creating a beautiful garden for you and the ones you love, you are bringing joy into your being.

You can also plant a real garden, big or small. Or bring into your space a few plants that you find pretty. This can be a powerful experience where you can connect to Mother Earth, care for another living thing, and provide the space for you to disconnect from negative thoughts and submerge yourself in your new harmonious space filled with grace.

Meditating and Connecting to Your Soul

If you have never meditated, I highly recommend trying. It is a great way to calm your body and quiet your mind. Again, this takes practice, time, and most importantly, patience with yourself. But I promise you it can be a very powerful and intimate experience.

There are many ways to meditate. There are guided meditations that can help you get started if you need them. These can be especially helpful on the harder days, when your thoughts are being especially loud or negative. These meditations can guide you to really focus in on your breathing, or even through a visualization, it can help take you out of your thought loop.

If the idea of starting meditation seems overwhelming, just focus on breathing, the very act of taking in the good and releasing the bad. Breathe in and breathe out. If you notice a thought taking over, you can recognize it and release it in the same way you breathe out. Do not be hard on yourself when the thoughts do break through. Thank yourself for all that you are doing to feel good. Feel gratitude in all you do for yourself. It's a work in progress.

For bonus material go to ...

Try beginning your meditation practice simply with 3 to 5 minutes every day. That is all you need! Then, when you are ready, try for up to 15 minutes a day, which is ideal. It may come more easily on some days than others. Remember, having kindness and self-love is the goal! With this in mind, enjoy the experience of being with yourself. See where it takes you!

I have come to a place where I love meditating and can even lose track of time. It's that time that I can quiet my mind and connect within and with God. I feel the bliss and the indescribable happiness in my heart. When you practice mindful meditation and observe your thoughts and feelings without reacting or judging, allowing yourself to be, you are integrating the body, mind, and spirit. This practice brought me love and peace to my inner self. My hope is that it will help support you in your grief and in overcoming life's challenges as they arise.

Meditation is a love pill for the soul!

Spirituality

**"Dare to love yourself
as if you were a rainbow
with gold at both ends."
– Aberjhani, author and poet**

For some people, prayer can also be a form of meditation. It is praying that helps them connect to God and find comfort as they are moved through the challenging stages of their grief. This brings me to the concept of spirituality.

Spirituality can mean different things to different people. When you start practicing mindfulness and connecting with your feelings, your mind, your body, and your soul, you are spiritually connecting to the experience that you are living in the present moment. I've taken part in many religious celebrations, and I enjoy them so much. The people gather and the space fills up quickly with good energy and cheer. It's so uplifting to also meet new people that are kind. Also, usually there is delicious food to share and enjoy.

Many people find comfort in their religion or faith when they are going through their grief, and this is so wonderful. Shortly after Mike and I started dating, we started going to church every Sunday together with our girls. It was his routine and I embraced it. This time is for praying and being thankful for the week and all the amazing things that I am enjoying, especially our family time together. After mass, we usually go to Brady's Fox, an Irish restaurant. This restaurant is one of the places that we truly enjoy, with delicious food and great conversations with Mr. Brady.

If you do not identify with any religion, it's okay too. I remember that Ed did not identify with any religion. He shared many memories of his childhood, and some were painful. He was raised by two parents who had different religious beliefs and who barely spoke with each other. He did not like it. He did not care which church he attended, he just wanted everybody to be together. Instead, he was given the choice of going with his mother or father to church. He chose his father. He saw religion as the division between his parents and him. He often said, "We are supposed to love and care for each other regardless of the religion that we identify ourselves with." However, every time we visited

For bonus material go to ...

Connecticut, he would stop at Taco Bell and would tell his daughter that every Sunday after church, he would go to Taco Bell to eat with his father. They ate in the parking lot each time.

Kaya said one day, "Daddy, why would you eat in the parking lot?"

I am not sure, Peanut... it was what he did, and I looked forward to that!

Navah said, "Daddy, what about if it was cold? What did your daddy do?"

We did the same; we ate our meal outside in the parking lot. Sometimes adults do things that children don't always understand, but we know that they always mean well.

So, after Ed's passing, when we go to visit his mother, we end up at Taco Bell. Then we take the food and eat it at his mom's place. This way, we celebrate both the grandfather my daughters never met and also share in this ritual that has transcended generations.

Learn to Connect with Yourself While Embracing the Memory and Treasuring the Moment

Connecting to your spirituality is also a way of dealing with everyday challenges in life and tapping into something greater than yourself. I believe that we are all connected. When I treat a person who comes into my life with love, kindness, and acceptance, seeing myself reflected in them, I am healing, raising my energy, and getting closer to my purpose in life. This is a wonderful feeling. It is also an experience that leads to self-awareness and the ability to monitor my own thoughts and feelings. When I do this, I am able to create experiences that guide my path in life and nourish my soul.

Seeing Ed's soul leave his body was an indescribable moment and part of my spiritual awakening. It was the bridge I crossed as I tried to understand what I had seen. I knew that Ed had passed on the message: "The soul goes on". This was Ed's gift to me when departing. He wanted to let me know that he was just changing forms—from the physical to the nonphysical. Ed did not die; he moved on to his next adventure for which he no longer needed his physical body.

I am able to feel Ed, and Maria as well. One day, I was driving to Connecticut with Kaya and Navah to visit Ed's mom, Sharon. Out of the blue, I heard myself say, "Ed, I bet that you are very happy that we are going to see your mom!"

In response, a song that he had dedicated to me started playing on the radio. I looked up to see a blue sky, and the only clouds around were forming Ed's name. Navah was in the passenger seat, and I said, "Navah, what do you see in the sky?"

"Mami, its Daddy's name! He is responding and letting us know that he is happy."

For bonus material go to ...

Sometimes I say, "Ed, give me a sign that you heard what I said, or give me a sign that you are near."

And sure enough, it happens; if not within seconds, within minutes. It's amazing.

"Ask and it will be given to you; see and you will find; knock and the door will be opened to you." Matthew 6:6

The Power of Integrating Mindfulness and Spirituality

As you integrate mindfulness into your daily life, it becomes a spiritual moment in time to hold and cherish. Each day, I find many things to be grateful for and mindful about. When a thought of Ed surfaces, I say, "Ed, thank you for being in my life for twelve years. I am a better person because of you. Thank you for bringing Kaya and Navah to my existence. Thank you for being there for me when we lost Kai. Thank you always for your unconditional love and support." This is a form of prayer...an intimate one.

"Prayer is the soul's sincere desire. Your desire is your prayer. It comes out of your deepest needs and it reveals the things you want in life."
— Joseph Murphy

www.griefandgratitudebook.com

Be Present

I am present during my interactions with my husband, Mike, who makes my heart sing. Mentally or verbally, I tell him how happy I am to have him in my life. I am more present when spending time with my daughters. This has led me to set aside time weekly, usually on Fridays, for "Mommy and Me" tea time.

During this time, we come home and gather at the dinner table or outside and enjoy a treat and a drink or an ice cream. The most important thing is that we gather together and have conversations with the intention to be present and listen to each other. At times, these conversations can be deep and emotional. The beauty of it is that they are released in a loving and safe space.

This is also an opportunity to pass on strategies that have worked for me. I am not sure if you have heard of *The Four Agreements* by Mexican author Don Miguel Ruiz. Let me tell you about them!

The four agreements are as follows:

- Agreement 1: Be impeccable with your word.
- Agreement 2: Don't take anything personally.
- Agreement 3: Don't make assumptions.
- Agreement 4: Always do your best.

Because these four agreements resonated so strongly with me, and it is the way I try to live my life, I usually refer to them when I am having conversations with my daughters. Not only do I talk about these agreements, but I also look to model them in my daily life. Your children learn more by what they see than by what you say. These four agreements have and continue to transform many of the experiences that I encounter by consciously choosing to use them.

Feel Better and Heal by Practicing Yoga

I joined the movement Breathe for Change. This is a training program for educators and leaders that focuses on wellness, yoga, and social-emotional learning. Yoga is a practice that focuses on physical and mental ways to connect the mind, body, and environment surrounding us. There are many different types of yoga. I usually practice Vinyasa yoga. It focuses on individual poses and deep breaths. I notice that when I practice yoga at home or take a class, I feel a great level of relaxation and sense of calm. In a nutshell, I feel great with one positive thought flowing after another. Yoga is seen to reduce anxiety and help with depression. If you want to challenge yourself, you can try Bikram yoga. The heat, the sweat, and the poses are great! During grief, it can help restore your energy and make you feel good.

You Are Worthy of a Magnificent Life

*"There are only two ways to live your life.
One is as though nothing is a miracle. The other is
as though everything is a miracle."*
– Albert Einstein

www.griefandgratitudebook.com

Ask yourself these questions:

- **I being mindful and consciously aware of the present moment?**
- **What is it that I want?**

Figuring out what you want can be the most challenging task. Therefore, setting goals can be hard if you do not know what you want or feel indecisive or even confused. This is normal, especially during grief. If this is your case, go to that intimate and quiet space you have chosen. You may want to decorate this space with beautiful plants (or whatever resonates with you), for meditation or praying. For me, this space is in one of the corners of my bedroom.

Through the corner window, I can admire a big and beautiful tree where birds gather to delight me with their songs. I have a small table with a pink crystal candle holder, a small Himalayan salt lamp, crystals, and pictures of angels that were given to me by my mentors, Charo Zamarron and Norma Uribe, for guidance and healing. I also have a small aqua-blue beetle and a small Statue of Liberty. These were both gifts from my mentor, Lupita Miguel, who does a lot of work with her clients' inner child, to help heal childhood trauma. She brought me the beetle from her trip to Egypt, and said, "Nancy, here is a symbol of the eternal cycle of life, the spirit, and it is now for you to keep."

I received the miniature Statue of Liberty during a Heaven and Earth retreat that I coordinated with my mentors. The aim was to work on breaking through the barriers of the past, while also embracing my current situation. The Statue of Liberty symbolizes freedom from suffering and the power of light that brightens my new path. I also have a meditation cushion. This space is very present in my life, and it's there upon rising and at the end of the day. It's also the space where I can feel at peace and be in touch with my inner self.

I ask for guidance and anything else I want from my teachers and the universe. I usually have conversations and I bring both of my hands to my heart: "God, thank you for being here with me. I am so grateful for my life. I thank you for my health and my family. Thank you for guiding my path and covering me with your love."

Three years ago, I asked myself what it was that I wanted. After spending some time in silence, praying and meditating, I had a feeling that I wanted to share my story with you. I started brainstorming and had lots of ideas. I began giving strong attention to my feelings, thoughts, and the healing process. The desire to write this book surfaced in December 2021. It was the perfect timing to start "the pregnancy" of my book, as one of my colleagues, Mrs. Edwards stated after I shared my idea of writing a book: "Nancy, writing a book is a great idea! See it as a pregnancy that is developing month by month and then is physically there to hold and share."

Then I thought, "This would be perfect! In 9 months, I can write and produce this book," which became one of my goals. I wrote it down and started this wonderful process of becoming an author. Most importantly, I am sharing the message that you can be happy again and that adversity is part of everyone's reality. If

www.griefandgratitudebook.com

I was able to move through my grief, you can also work through anything and find meaning in life.

Suffering is a choice. You do not have to choose it. I did not need to suffer, but I did need to learn ways to live with the loss of my son Kai. I needed to learn to live without Ed in my life. I needed to learn how to live as a widow and single mother.

I realized that the more conscious I was, the better prepared I felt. This mindfulness helped me find strategies to move through my grief, accept it, and learn how to live with it.

Moving forward was not forgetting, but rather developing, the ability to integrate the new feeling of loss into my life. The feeling of loss will never go away. As far as I know, it will always be part of who I am. It's a part of my journey in this life. You may be feeling the same way. If you are not, that's okay too. Your experience is unique to you and your journey.

Awareness Exercise

"Take your attention away from your problem and the multitude of reasons why you cannot achieve your ideal. Concentrate your attention entirely upon the thing desired."
– Neville Goddard

To end this chapter, I would like you to think again about what it is that you want to integrate into your new life. What legacy do you want to leave?

For bonus material go to ...

Or ask yourself, would I be okay with the way things are in my life now, in a year or two? How about in five years from now? If the answer is NO, you can change it by deciding where you want to focus your attention. Once you do that, you will get more of what you want. It begins with being mindful of the moment. Try to recognize what works and doesn't work for you. Dig deep and listen. What do you want to bring more of to your life? Remember, you may complete as many or as few of these exercises based on what resonates with you. They are optional and are always available to come back to at a later time.

1. Write down three goals you want to accomplish today. (I suggest getting a notebook or a calendar with space to practice goal setting daily.)

_____
_____
_____
_____

2. Use your time wisely and focus on what really matters to you and your family. Write about where you are spending your time in the day (e.g., spending time with loved ones, meditating, exercising, preparing healthy meals, organizing and cleaning, going on social media, or watching TV).

_____
_____
_____
_____

3. Do these activities bring you joy? Do they feed your life purpose? If not, write about how you can change that. What do you want to be spending your time on?

_____
_____
_____
_____

4. Are you making decisions on what feels right or based on what others want or expect you to do? Do not give your power to anyone unless you choose to. Be respectful but clear about what you would and would not accept from others. Is there something you want to do in your life, which you feel you have been holding back from doing because you don't think you should or because others will judge you?

_____
_____
_____
_____

5. Accept, respect, and love yourself for who you are! You are beautiful and don't have to change to please anyone. If you decide to change anything, it is because you are doing it for you.

One thing I love about myself is:

_____

For bonus material go to ...

One thing that I want to change about myself is:

_____
_____
_____
_____
_____

6. If you don't have anything positive to say, don't say anything. Be mindful of the recurring phrases you are using out of habit and analyze what they mean. If you conclude that you are not happy with what you are saying, find ways to rephrase and say what you want in a manner that empowers you.

What is a negative phrase you say to yourself or others?

_____
_____
_____
_____
_____

How would you rephrase it?

_____
_____
_____
_____
_____

www.griefandgratitudebook.com

7. Act on your hunches; they may be guiding you to your heart's desire. Write about your heart's truest desire. (Try using bullets; you may need more than five lines!)

_____
_____
_____
_____
_____

8. Go to sleep tonight thinking positive thoughts. Write or think about five things you are grateful for and focus on your breath. Keep breathing…sweet dreams.

_____
_____
_____
_____
_____

9. Write things down; do not rely on your memory!

This last one helped me tremendously by putting ideas on paper, carrying a calendar, and making weekly and daily lists. I prioritized the things I needed to accomplish each day. Whichever item(s) I was not able to do or finish became part of my list the next day. You can also write a note on your cell phone. Here is a spot for a few things that you'd like to remember for tomorrow. If you can't think of anything, write "breathe" to start.

For bonus material go to ...

_____
_____
_____
_____
_____

The Secret Is Out

Shhhhhh, do you want to know a secret? The more grateful you are, the better you will feel and the more you will find to be grateful for. This will raise your energy and you'll start to feel great. Accompany a morning gratitude practice with a short meditation upon standing, and as you begin to walk, you may feel that you are walking on a cloud and your heart is bursting with love. This has been my experience numerous times. And this is when I feel most blessed!

www.griefandgratitudebook.com

My Notes

For bonus material go to www.griefandgratitudebook.com

My Notes

Chapter 10
You Are Worthy!

"And the thing about blooming is, nothing about the process is easy. It requires every part of you to stretch upward, with your roots firmly planted in the ground; and in the sun, and in the rain, and wind, you stand anyway, even against the pull of the soil. And through it all, one day you will see all along you were transforming."
– Morgan Harper Nichols

10

My Wish to YOU

From my heart to yours, I wish you a smooth transition from where you are to where you are meant to be in your life. As your awareness and desire to live a happier and more fulfilled life increases, let this be the steppingstone to a life filled with endless possibilities. Life may appear complex, but it does not have to be. As you decide on what makes your soul sing, eliminate anything that does not serve you or moves you closer to your goals, and desires. You have all it takes to go through your transformations. Take it at a steady pace and enjoy each step you take in becoming the best you-your "other self." Believe you can, and you have the power to manifest all your dreams for your highest good and for those around you and the world.

Things to Remember

Turbulent Times Come and Go

As you integrate your grief into your life, you will go through turbulence. This may go on for quite some time. Keep in mind that not only death but also other life-changing events can impact you significantly. It's important to see these times as part of being alive. Your human experience is part of your life journey on Earth.

For bonus material go to ...

Each obstacle you overcome will teach you a lesson and can even lead to a transformation.

Many times, these events are unexpected and change the course of your ship. With or without your consent, they will push you out of your comfort zone onto an unpredictable path. Each turbulence that you experience can cause pain, discomfort, and leave you out of breath. Remember, regardless of their intensity, they will pass. Do not see them as a punishment for something you have done wrong in your life, but rather an opportunity to let your soul shine bright and reach your unlimited self.

Refocus Your Lens

In college, I was given a nickname, "Nancy Pictures." Photography is one of my hobbies. I find it fascinating to be able to capture a moment in time as I am experiencing it. I enjoy taking photos of nature, interesting sites, gatherings, and children at play. In a nutshell, I like taking pictures of anything I find beautiful.

What do I do if I take a picture that I do not like? Well, I delete it and take another one! I only keep those images that touch my heart. I hold the memory and appreciate being part of the moment. At times, when I go back to the photos I have taken, I notice that I also capture other images that I never intended to; such as lights, insects, people in the background, etc. I've been amazed with things I have captured.

I have found that the lessons I learned in my photography also connect to life in general. Focus on what you want and on the photo you want to take. Learn from the experience as you go through it. If the picture you have does not resonate with you, refocus your lens, change the scenery, and snap another one. Keep doing this until you are satisfied with your life picture and what you see through your lens. Knowing that you have the choice to delete or keep your current picture is empowering.

When You Accept Dying, It's Liberating

After losing Ed, I think about death often, even though it now seems like a distant event. The truth of the matter is that I don't know when my turn will be. I have moved through the fear of dying and have accepted it. I now know that my soul will continue the journey.

Just like me, you may also be having more thoughts about death and dying after losing your loved one. This is perfectly normal as you focus on your current situation while also trying to move through your grief and find purpose in life.

Regardless of how you view a death, you have an opportunity to refocus and view it from a different perspective. For me, Ed's death was both a wake-up call and an opportunity to refocus my lens on myself. This is how life events can be viewed once you see them for what they are: a photo that can be deleted without getting your feelings involved, because you know you can always take another one.

I will forever be thankful to Ed, for it took me seeing his soul leave his body for my spiritual awakening to take place. I learned that there is more to dying than what I knew. You may be realizing

For bonus material go to ...

by now that you, like me, had a transformational experience that was only possible because you went through a crisis first.

There Is Healing in Sharing Your Story

Don't be afraid to openly share your story when you are ready to do so. Don't bury the pain, rather, embrace this new beginning with acceptance and grace. Talk about the things that your loved one did that made you feel special, happy, and filled with love. Also, share the things that "got under your craters" and have a good laugh!

Remembering and sharing your loved one's story shows appreciation for the memories and tells others about who they were. As you know, sharing is caring. When you share, you are providing that intimate yet vulnerable space for others to do the same. When you do this, true healing "bursts," reaching those with whom you are communicating.

Honoring Your Grief is Healing

I invite you to not only honor your loved one as discussed previously but also the grief that is a result of the loss. This can be challenging at first. Trust me, you can do it; or you may be doing it already. Surrendering and accepting your grief is honoring it. When you surrender, you let go of the need to control everything that is around you and others. Surrendering is trusting that God's plan is perfect even when you cannot see how that is possible.

This is what happened to me. This is why I am sharing my story with you. I was where you are at this moment: once with the loss of my son and once again with the loss of my husband. In one of my prayers, I said, "God, you love me so much that when I lost my son and my husband, you gave me three other souls to love unconditionally and to cherish. Not to mention Papa Mike and Maureen, Mike's parents, who are as loving and caring as my own parents and their wonderful families."

It's your loss and your grief. Honoring it makes you stronger. It gives you the strength you need to transform what you are feeling into the motivation that fuels you to keep appreciating the life that you still have. It also helps you accept new changes and welcome new experiences. When you honor, respect, and value your grief, the love you feel for the departed loved ones helps you to openly and courageously mourn and accept your circumstances. This is life transforming and it empowers you to help others by sharing your story.

Start Feeling Whole and in Alignment

As we are coming to the end of this book, I want to share my own personal view on the importance of feeling whole as you are going through a transformation as a result of having experienced a crisis or traumatic event in your life. In my case, losing Ed was the beginning of my spiritual transformation. My view on this topic may be different from yours, and it's perfectly okay. We are all different and will have different stories.

For me, accepting my grief and healing was part of my spiritual transformation as well as the connection to my physical and spiritual worlds. Everything was interconnected and there was no

For bonus material go to ...

separation. When I meditate or pray, I feel connected to my source, the Universe, God, or whatever you believe in that is greater than you. I am calm, at peace. I feel aligned and whole.

Embracing my spiritual journey helped me to see that everything has a reason. It's like seeing your life's puzzle pieces being connected right in front of you. My wish is that you can come to the realization that the part of you that you thought was gone when you lost your loved one, never really left you. With this realization, you can begin to feel worthy and joyful. You will be able to start to welcome love into your life and you will realize that you have everything you need within you to be happy. Love is the key ingredient to a fulfilled life.

> **"An authentically powered person lives in love. Love is the energy of the soul. Love is what heals the personality. There is nothing that cannot be healed by love. There is nothing but love."**
> **— Gary Zukav**

Only the Surfer Knows the Feeling!

When I started to integrate my mind, body, soul, and spirit, I became more aware of my surroundings, my thoughts, my body, and my prayers. I started meditating regularly. I became interested in places I had visited but had never noticed the details, colors, shapes, etc. I knew answers to questions, and I didn't know where the information was coming from.

I started tapping into the energy around me and reading it to the point that I would pick up others' energy. Sometimes, I knew what other people were going to say before they said it. This was an epiphany because I learned that all I needed to do was to focus and ask, "What do I need to learn here?" or "Why am I having this interaction?"

Sometimes, out of nowhere, I felt the urge to convey a message to someone. At times, I would have the thought, "That's silly," but it was immediately followed by another thought, "Give the message." So, I would; and at times, the person receiving the message would cry and say, "Thank you so much. That was the answer to my prayer." Or the person with tears in their eyes would ask me if they could give me a hug, and they would thank me many times.

Rarely but sometimes, a person would ask, "How do you know that?" I would simply say, "I don't know; I just know," leaving the person puzzled. To my surprise, each time this happened, I felt the love expanding in my heart. It was a magical feeling.

Sometimes I would have a dream with a message to pass on. After a long time, I started remembering my dreams. I am not questioning why this was happening to me; it just was. And I loved this feeling because I felt the love and I had the opportunity to bring comfort to another person.

As I thought more and more about this, I realized that I am enjoying paddling to catch the waves of life, but most importantly, I have fun riding them. As Ed would say, "Amore, only the surfer knows the feeling!"

For bonus material go to ...

Listen to Your Mind, Body, Soul, and Spirit

Mind: At the beginning, I was constantly asking myself, "Am I watching my thoughts and only holding onto the ones that bring me joy? Or am I entertaining negative thoughts that bring my energy down with low frequencies? Or am I being kept busy by creating stories that are only happening in my mind?

I consciously check in with my thoughts and only entertain those that I choose to. Remember that you have the power to change a negative thought to a positive one in a second. Notice what the thought is and observe it. Is it the same recurrent thought? Identify each thought and ask yourself, "Does it serve me now?" If the answer is "No!" the next time it reappears, acknowledge it, thank it, and see it fading like a bubble. Sayonara! Be consistent in using this strategy, and you will notice that these recurring thoughts will fade away just like bubbles.

Body: Am I listening to my body? What is my body telling me at this moment? Get to know your body and your feelings.

Ask yourself: "How do I feel now?" It's possible that you might realize in that moment you are actually feeling okay when you thought you shouldn't be. You recognize that you are in a safe place and are surrounded by many things that bring joy to your experience. Maybe it is that you have food to eat and clean water to drink. You have a shelter that protects you at night. You have a bed and a warm blanket. There is much to be grateful for in the physical world.

Soul: As I understand it, it is the part of me that guides and protects. My soul gives life to my personality and keeps me going during this physical experience called life. While in this physical experience, I can use all my senses to experience the world around me. My soul is the candle and guiding force within me that will continue to live on even when my body's time has come to an end. My understanding may be different from yours.

Spirit: My spirit is my connection to all that is and it allows me to communicate with God within. It's that part of me that when I pray or meditate, confirms that I am part of something greater. This greater power is pure love. This love connects us to all that is. I am part of the whole. My goal is to try to feel and give more love to myself, my family, and everyone who crosses my path.

Learn the Lesson

I realized that I did all I could to help Ed heal and return home. Unfortunately, it did not happen as I had hoped. It's hard to believe what I experienced when he decided to release his body and depart from the physical plane. I remember being overwhelmed by one question after the other: Did I see his soul because I was ready for the experience? Or because this was the goodbye he chose to give me? Could anyone else watching have seen his soul leave his body?

My mother and my brother, Pedro were there. However, they did not see what I saw. After going back and forth, I have come to the realization that all the experiences I have and will encounter in this lifetime were meant to be. It's my script.

For bonus material go to ...

Your attitude impacts the way you play your role. I learned that when I do the best I can, there is no regret, guilt, or shame. There is only acceptance and lessons learned. I see everyone who comes into my life as my teacher. Even my daughters are some of my greatest teachers! Each situation I mindfully encounter, I often ask:

- What is it that I need to learn from this situation?
- What is the lesson here that I need to learn to heal my soul?

I try not to take things personally. Sometimes the lesson is obvious, and at other times, I have to reflect a little longer on the entire experience, or I will figure it out as I go. I am still learning, changing, and transforming as I continue to go through my life path one day at a time. I understand that I am becoming my best self, filled with love and kindness. I am not apart from, but a part of, everything.

Live and Say *Yes* to Your Best Life

Living your best life is sustaining the feeling that you are worthy of a magnificent life, welcoming joy and feeling gratitude for your experience in this life.

When you say *yes* to life, it's because you realize that you have everything you need to be happy and to feel love within, for yourself and for those around you. Self-love is the greatest gift you can give yourself. This is especially true while grieving and being vulnerable.

Healing Tools

When you allow yourself to feel worthy of a magnificent life, you will begin to give yourself time to heal. You'll take the time you need for physical, emotional, and spiritual healing. To end this book, I want to share with you a few more things I do for myself regularly.

Oils and Some of Their Healing Properties

As I previously mentioned, I carry essential oils with me. I use coconut oil for everything. Every day, I use it on my body, and at night I use it on my face and on Mike's face as well. It's great for massages, and you can combine it with other oils of your choice. It's also wonderful for your hair. If my daughters get a cut or have pain anywhere on their body, I use raw, virgin, cold-pressed coconut oil. I also take advantage of the many health benefits of the coconut as a food and drink.

I pour lavender oil into my diffuser when I pray, meditate, or practice yoga. Not only do I love the smell of lavender, but it's also calming and soothing.

I apply eucalyptus oil when I feel congested or when my daughters have a cold. I rub a bit on their chest with coconut oil. Eucalyptus is another favorite of mine. I add a few drops to hand cream, shower gel, and so on. It has anti-inflammatory properties, which can alleviate pain and aid in healing. I spray it in the bathroom before taking a shower.

For bonus material go to ...

If you come to my house, you will find a small bottle of peppermint spray in every restroom. It's great for keeping the restroom smelling fresh and minty!

I also love the smell of rose oil. I use it on my wrist in the mornings to help maintain my happy mood and reduce any feelings of anxiety.

I use sandalwood to maintain my focus for the day and aid in calming my nerves. This really helps, especially if you are meeting people for the first time, participating in an event, or speaking in public.

Take a Healing Bath and Reconnect to Your Inner Power

These types of baths are my favorite, and I want to share them with you. A healing bath is perfect when you are feeling heavy or uneasy. It brings harmony, peace, and rejuvenation to your being. You can also set one up for your children. My daughters love healing baths. We have them on special occasions. They do take time and should not be rushed.

Healing Bath Steps – This is how I do it. You may want to replace some of the ingredients to suit your needs or based on what you have available. I start by bringing all the ingredients to the restroom. This is best done in a bathtub.

Step 1: Prepare a healthy snack.

Get a small bowl with berries, a mandarin, or other healthy snacks with a glass of water. Bring it to the space where you will take your healing bath, and leave it on the side.

Step 2: Prepare the bathtub.

Clean and fill your bathtub with hot/warm water. Add any 100% essential oils of your choice, rose petals, and a few drops of eucalyptus oil to the water. Then add a spoon of raw honey. Bring a small candle and matches. Set your intentions as you are adding the ingredients to the bathtub. For example, put your hand over the water and say: "Calm, joy, energy, clarity, love, creativity, guidance, healing, acceptance…"

If you wish for a partner, set your intentions for the person that you want to welcome into your life. When we are looking for that other half, it's important to think about what you are ready to give and the commitment that you would like to make. It's important to think about the qualities that you are bringing and know that those are the ones that will be matched. A relationship is a give and take.

Step 3: Prepare yourself.

Once your bath is set, bring a bowl or container with two full cups of water into the space (you can add more water if you like), two spoons of raw coconut oil, and add two handfuls of rose petals and two teaspoons of cinnamon. (I usually buy fresh flowers. I keep two, and use the others' petals for the bath.) You will need a

For bonus material go to ...

shower gel and raw brown sugar. Also, bring a spoon to scoop the sugar from the container into the palm of your hands.

Make sure your phone is off. I usually play music for meditation and relaxation. At this stage, it's important that you are connected to yourself and not distracted.

Think about what it is that you want to release and get rid of during this experience (sadness, confusion, uncertainty, negative thoughts, illness, etc.).

Turn on the shower. Get yourself wet from head to toe. Feel the water as it falls on each part of your body, starting with your head and moving downward to your feet and the shower floor.

Turn off the water. Put a spoonful of raw sugar and some shower gel into your hands. Reach out to the container that has the water, coconut, rose petals, and cinnamon. Start cleaning your being. Start with your head, face, and keep moving down to your feet. Feel the love in your hands, feel the sugar and the sensory stimulation provided by the gel, sugar, petals, etc. Enjoy the smell of these ingredients as you clean your head and body with them. Enjoy the experience. Do it twice. You don't need to put too much on your face.

Then turn the shower back on and visualize that as the ingredients are being washed away from your body, so are those things that you want to release. See them leave your body from head to toe as you scan your body and the water is rinsing you. Once you have finished rinsing, come out and dry yourself.

Step: 4: Prepare to receive your healing.

Get a match or lighter and a .5-inch candle. Here you need to restate your intentions for the healing bath one more time. You can write your intentions for a more powerful experience. At this stage, I am usually feeling lighter, my energy is rising, and I can feel it moving all over my body.

Light the candle and get in the bathtub. Relax, accept, and receive the healing. Use your senses to mindfully enjoy the experience. Feel the worthiness with each part of your body. This is a quiet time. Receive the healing; breathe. Focus on breathing. Accept any emotion that surfaces and let it out. Give yourself around 45 minutes to an hour here.

Step 5: Feel the gratitude and give thanks three times for whatever you are most grateful for and repeat this affirmation:

"God is the source of my supply. His riches flow to me freely, copiously, and abundantly. All my financial and other needs are met at every moment of time and point of space; there is always a divine surplus."
– Dr. Joseph Murphy

Get out, dry yourself and get comfortable. Sit and eat your snack, enjoying the experience and feeling the gratitude and love in your heart. Keep visualizing exactly what you want at details to your mind picture.

Once you are done if you feel like taking a nap, feel free to do so and relax.

For bonus material go to ...

There is no limit to the healing baths you can do weekly. It's up to you. I do them when I am having a challenging week or time in my life and need healing, guidance, and clarity. I did it often during the first three months after losing Ed.

Questions to frequently ask yourself:

1. What do I want to leave in the past?
2. What do I want to see as a result of my transformation?

For the first question: Think about and make a list of what no longer serves you. Once you have made this list, I recommend that you become aware of the behaviors, thinking patterns and feelings that you are consciously choosing not to bring into your new reality. This can also be people who are not having a positive impact on your life and that you want to break from or limit your interactions with. You can keep adding to your list as needed.

Your response to question 1: What do I want to leave in the past?

- _____
- _____
- _____
- _____
- _____
- _____
- _____

What do I want to see as a result of my transformation or my new reality?

Write it down; be clear and specific and see yourself there. Feel the joy in your heart as you visualize it and see your end result. Do not dwell on the things that are negatively affecting you in your current situation as this will only be an obstacle in getting to your destination. Therefore, it is best to focus on the end result, your final goal. Each day, set up small objectives and take actions to move closer to your end goal.

You can add, change and take away from your list at any given time. It's perfectly okay to keep changing it until you have your perfect list. Don't worry about how you will get the things on your list. Feel good about the process of thinking and writing down the things you desire. Once your list is done, memorize it! I rewrote my list a few times. Do not type your list, write it down with pen or pencil and paper. Don't skip the step of writing it down. This helps in imprinting your list to your subconscious, the part of the mind which you are not fully aware, but has a major influence on your thoughts and feelings. Then, refer to your list often during the day. My favorite times to see my list are in the morning and before bedtime. Going to sleep thinking about your list is powerful. These thoughts and happy and excited feelings become like a magnet attracting what you want into your physical reality. And sooner, rather than later, you will start to notice small changes in your life that are pleasant. These are also called synchronicities, the simultaneous occurrence of events which appear significantly related but have no discernible causal connection.

For bonus material go to ...

Be aware that you might see your situation getting worse before it gets better. These disruptions or temporary chaos that may manifest in your life are part of the bigger picture as your life is restructuring at all levels. See these situations as your new road being paved for your transformation and allow the person that you are becoming to take form.

Your response to question 2: What do I want to see as a result of my transformation or what do I want in my life?

- _____
- _____
- _____
- _____
- _____
- _____
- _____
- _____

If you are unsure as to what it is that you truly want, ask yourself: In six months or in one year, would I be okay if I am still where I am today?

Your answer will guide you in discovering what brings joy to your heart. Knowing what you want to accomplish is the key to obtaining it and the first step to your transformation.

www.griefandgratitudebook.com

Here is a guide that you can use to set up daily short-term goals.

Daily To-Do List (can look something like this):

Date: _____

I Am Talented! Today, with grace and ease, I will accomplish:
_____

- _____
- _____
- _____
- _____

I Triumph! Today's top short term goals are: I am a goal getter!
_____

- _____
- _____
- _____
- _____

I Am Terrific! I give and I receive with ease. Today, I am grateful for: _____

- _____
- _____
- _____
- _____

For bonus material go to ...

I am Worthy and the Warrior of My Own Life

I am worthy and the warrior of my own life
Accepting myself just the way I am

I am worthy and the warrior of my life
You and I are linked tight

I am worthy and the warrior of my life
Harmoniously accepting that earth and I are one

I am worthy and the warrior of my own life
Guiding myself with positive thoughts and a kind heart

I am worthy and the warrior of my own life
For my own happiness, I go deep inside,
for I possess all I need for a joyful life

I am worthy and the warrior of my own life
For the answers that I seek, I can find by connecting
to my higher self, my guide

I am worthy and the warrior of my own life
For I am made perfect and complete and there is no one like me

I am worthy and the warrior of my own life
And when I fall, I rise again, stepping forward
without blame or shame

I am worthy and the warrior of my own life
I will always have my back, protect, and love who I am

www.griefandgratitudebook.com

I am worthy and the warrior of my own life
Letting my light shine bright as I follow my path and discover my purpose this time

I am worthy and the warrior of my own life
I was made from the one above with unconditional love
To create, experience, and thrive in this experience we all call life.

Be You, Be Well, Be Kind
I love you just the way you are, for you and I are one.

By Nancy Jalowiecki Sullivan

For bonus material go to ...

As I color this mandala, I am unleashing my full potential to become who I am. I am letting my light shine. Enjoy this moment.

Stay Connected

It is time to give yourself a loving hug and congratulate yourself for all of the work you are doing to live in your purpose and to step into your magnificent life. If you enjoyed the work we did together in this book and want to learn more about how we can continue to work together, you can find my offerings on my website, griefandgratitude.com.

www.griefandgratitudebook.com

My Notes

For bonus material go to www.griefandgratitudebook.com

My Notes

Acknowledgements

Mike, thank you for your ongoing support and unconditional love, especially in the process of writing this book. Thank you also for encouraging me every step of the way. I am so grateful for all the weekends you watched over our daughters so that I could focus on my writing. I love you so much, tesoro mio.

A big thank you to my four caring and loving daughters, *Kaya, Navah, Molly, and Keeva,* for being my reminder that adversity is a period of rebirth, and for allowing me to enjoy so many happy moments felt deep in my heart. You are my teachers and my motivation to continue to live life to the fullest. Your independence allowed me to spend more time writing. I appreciate and enjoy our "Mommy and Me" tea time gatherings.

To my mom, *Margarita,* for your love and all the sacrifices you made to give me a better life, and for all the love and prayers you send my way each and every day.

To my father, *Papa Juan,* and my stepmom, *Mama Deny,* for your love and guidance. Mama Deny, I can't wait to have some of your rice and beans y cafecito and celebrate with you both. Papi, I am sending you healing thoughts.

For bonus material go to ...

A big hug to my siblings, *Ceci, Marisol, Glenny, Endy, Carmen, Ester,* and *Johnny,* and their families, for the beautiful times we have shared and for all the love that only those close to your heart can feel.

To all my nieces and nephews, Titi loves you all very much.

Francia Ortiz and family, thank you for being you, and for loving me unconditionally and proving to me that I can count on you for anything! I am here for you. I love you. I could not have asked for a better life sister than you.

Mark, Elba, Maddox, and *Mason,* I love you and I thank you for being in our lives. Thank you for saying "yes" to caring for our four daughters if need be. You do not know how much this meant to Ed and now to Mike and me. Elba, I enjoyed sharing a cup of coffee and catching up at Starbucks. Thank you for listening to my ideas for this book. Mark, Ed called you my brother from another mom, and that is exactly what you are: a brother in our lives and an uncle to our daughters.

Padrino *Scott, Kelly, Sydney* and *Saige,* thank you for being there for Ed and me and the girls unconditionally. Scott, for Ed, you were his older brother. He loved you so much and enjoyed sharing childhood memories with me. Thank you for always having his back.

Kelly, thank you for being my mentor and my friend. I love you.

Marlene Jimenez (*Ruby*), thank you for leaving your family in Florida to come to New York City, without knowing me, and helping us with the girls and Panchito during the most difficult time of my life. You'll forever have a special place in my heart. *Robert*, in you, I found a friend and brother. Ruby could not have found a better person than you to share her life with. I am sending you and your family my love.

Yenie, Ramona, Susana, and Damaris, I care and have so much love for each of you. You probably know me better than anyone and I thank you for your love and support each step of the way. I cherish our time together.

Thank you, *Cecilia,* for being the perfect au pair match for our family. *Oscar* and *Zulema,* thank you for confirming one more time that there is magic and connection in each one of us with God's greatest gift, love. Your gift, *Tarija Magica* by Therese Ide Tity, warmed my heart. I can't wait to visit Tarija, Bolivia, and meet your family in person and visit some of these places illustrated in the book.

Thank you, Anna Sophie, for your big heart. Your parents, John and Karin, have done an amazing job raising such a responsible, organized and caring daughter. You're the perfect example for Lisa Marie, who will always look up to you, her big sister. It was so easy to provide you with coaching and guidance during your visit to America because having no expectation brings magic to our life and experiences. It is a pleasure to have you in our lives, and to be part of your life journey.

For bonus material go to ...

Thank you, cousin *Jeff, Jennifer, Joe, Becca, Aillie, Paxton, Lauren,* and *Dorian,* and the rest of the *Jalowiecki* family, for being there for us through the good and bad times. I am very grateful to have you in my life and for your support throughout the years.

Ed: "Mom, look at my wife; she looks like an angel, wouldn't you agree? Look how beautiful she looks..."

Ed's mom, Sharon: "I've seen some better-looking blondies!"

Sharon, I may not be a blondie, but I love you with all my heart. I thank you for being part of my life journey and for sharing your son with me. I am glad that I can be here for you unconditionally. You lost your son but have gained a daughter in me. And yes, I will bring you a copy of this book, signed!

Thank you, Uncle Jimmy, Aaron, and Chris for your love and ongoing support. Thank you also for the delicious meals you always prepared for us. I am sending you all a big hug.

I am so fortunate to have *Maureen* and *Mike Sullivan* and their beautiful daughters, *Colleen, Erin, Joanne,* and *Chrissy,* and their families and friends, in my life. Colleen, thank you for welcoming me to the family. I'll never forget the thoughtful engagement dinner that you had for us. Erin, thank you for being my maid of honor and helping to make our wedding so special. Joanne, thank you for taking the long trips up from Delaware to celebrate with us. Chrissy, thank you for all the work you are doing to promote cultural awareness and inclusivity with your work with the Long Branch Arts and Cultural Center. I was honored to have the opportunity to contribute my art to the Hispanic Heritage celebration. Thank you all for welcoming the girls and me with open arms into your family. I am very grateful for all the traveling and the ongoing support and help with our daughters. *Nanny* and *Papa Mike,* I am honored to be part of your beautiful and caring family. The welcoming dinner with your siblings and friends was so special. It warms my heart when Kaya tells me that she can't wait to visit Aunt Kathy in New Mexico and spin yarn on her spinning wheel. I enjoyed being part of Doris's 100 (and a half!) birthday celebration with so many caring and wonderful family members.

Michael and *Diana,* it's with a heart full of love that I thank you both for accepting and welcoming my daughters and me into your life. Uncy, thank you for taking your time to teach, play, and love all your nieces unconditionally.

Eron and *Bill,* thank you for keeping in touch and showing how much you care about the girls. Ed appreciated your ongoing love and support while in the hospital and had so much love for you both, as well as for *Tyler,* whom he always referred to as his younger brother.

Peter Kuehbauch, Ed and I enjoyed our time together. He admired your free spirit and enjoyed creating music with you, Jimmy and Kevin.

Peter Sanatore, Ed was so happy for you, Alice and your children. I can hear his laughter while carrying on and playing with your daughter in your backyard.

For bonus material go to ...

Querida Evie, you have been one of the guiding angels in my life. Thank you for being part of my energy family and for always being there for me and for suggesting the tittle of this book. I love you.

Leah Dimond, Carmen Peña, Haydee Flores, Marlene Lizardo, and *Diomery Sanchez,* thank you for you friendship and for your unconditional love. I love you and I am grateful for our friendship throughout the years.

Jackie Garcia, Yasmin Olivero, Johanna and *Nico,* thank you for being beautiful souls and part of my energy family. Nico, your visit to the hospital meant so much to us. Thank you for sharing and caring.

Maria and *Rafael Vargas,* my adopted parents in this life, thank you for treating me as your own daughter and for all the prayers you sent my way, when prayer was my only hope.

Jenny and Chris Mairhofer, and family, I love you and appreciate your ongoing support. My sister from my adopted parents. Thank you for sending us information about grieving and living. Thank you for your unbelievable hospitality and generosity and making me feel at home in Austria.

Judy Almanzar and *Pedro Vargas* and family, thank you for reaching out, for showing that you care, and for the great conversations and love we shared. Judy, I am grateful for the healing and energy bracelet you gave me.

www.griefandgratitudebook.com

Tony Vargas, thank you for showing that you care and for all the love you sent my way.

Preciosa Arelis, I am thinking of you and sending you a big, warm and loving hug.

Elida, Teresa, and *Mota,* I have so much love for you all. Thank you for your love and friendship; I am grateful for our conversations about life, love, and intimacy.

To my caring and loving aunts, *Utri, Griselda, Germania, Lala, Francia, Mary, Gracita, Diosa,* and *Zula,* as well as my uncles, *Francisco, Leoner, Eusebio, Juan,* and *Cirilo,* and your families, for your guidance and support throughout my life. I love you all.

Rosemary, Lully, Alba, Carmen, Yuri, Ines, Tago, Maritza, Janet, Joici, Dania, Millie, Lisa, Lola, Juri, Lorisa, Erika, Dilenia, Giselle, Iris, Alba, and *Barbara S,* I love you and thank you for being in my life. We all got a trait from our beautiful grandmas, Mama Merced and Mama Eliza that guides and remind us that sharing is caring.

Thank you to all my handsome cousins and their families, especially *Santiago, Tony M. Miguel Angel, Robin, Roberto, David, Marcos, Charlie, Cirilito, Tony F., David F., Melvin, Jeffrey, Juancito, Chelo, Erik, Jony, Jean Carlos,* and *Jose Antonio,* for your love and support. I really appreciate your hugs filled with love.

For bonus material go to ...

Marisol, Madeline, Cristina, and *Jackie*, thank you for your kindness and support. You are so beautiful and such kind neighbors, who showed me that your neighbors become your family in time of need. Thank you for caring for Kaya and Navah when I needed it the most. Because of your kindness, I was able to spend more time with Ed in his final days.

Lorraine Puello, Leo and *Esmeralda*, thank you for loving and taking care of Kaya and Navah as your own daughters. You have a special place in my heart. Thank you for religiously setting up a day once a month to allow Ed and I to go out and celebrate our love. Ed loved you so much and appreciated your hugs.

Thank you, *Divina,* for caring for Kaya and Navah and for giving unconditional love to all the children you work with, and for making a difference in their lives and in our community.

Thank you to the incredible school community of *P.S. 98, the Magnet School of STEAM Studies,* and my second home. Ms. Rodriguez, Ms. Sanchez, Ms. Morelli, Ms. Hall, Ms. Bonifacio, Ms. Zavala, Ms. Mercado, Ms. Benitez, Ms. Dilone, and my colleagues, staff, and families: I am blessed with the love, support, and flexibility you wrapped me with. You all came together to make sure that I had the time that I needed to be by Ed's side when he needed me the most. With my heart filled with love and gratitude, I will always remember your kindness, compassion, and generosity.

Ms. Medina, thank you for checking up on me daily or each time you knew that I was with Ed. Thank you for the kind words and prayers and for showing me how much you care. You're a role model and one of my chosen mentors! I love you.

Ms. Rodriguez, Ms. Feliz, Ms. Paulino, Ms. Henriquez, Ms. De La Cruz, Ms. Cruz, Ms. Prado, Ms. Penny, and the rest of the paraprofessionals who gathered together in the teacher's lounge to pray for Ed's health and the stability of my family, thank you, thank you, thank you for your love.

Ms. Cabezas, Ms. Marte, Ms. Santos, Ms. Budhwa, Ms. Evans, Ms. Mendez, and *Mrs. Edwards,* you've been some of my greatest teachers. Thank you for your guidance, support, and love. I've learned so much from all of you.

Ms. Rosario, thank you for caring for Kaya and Navah and for allowing me to go see Ed at the hospital and spend quality time with him. I miss your beautiful smile filled with joy and life.

Ms. Peña, thank you for listening and for the emotional support you gave me when my world was turning upside down. Thank you for your kind and loving heart.

Annie, Andres, Raul, and JJ, your prayers touched my soul. Thank you for being such beautiful people inside and out. Your family will always have a special place in my heart.

To my *families, students, mentoring* and *coaching clients,* thank you for trusting in me and for being one of my greatest motivations to keep learning, and for reaching into our unlimited potential together, with grace and acceptance.

For bonus material go to ...

The amazing school community of *Muscota New School*, for going over and beyond expectations to make sure that the girls and I were okay, and for allowing Lucilla to bring Kaya and Navah to the hospital just in time to say goodbye to their daddy on the day of his passing. Special thanks to Camille, Ali, Susana, Marilyn, Hanin, Jean, Denise, Katherine, Monique, Ms. Mona, Heidi, and all the caring staff. This world is a better place because of people like you.

Ahna, Kristen, Sarah, Karen, Tracey, Laura, Anna, Katherine, and *Lucilla,* and their families, for being there for my family and I when we needed you the most. Thank you for your caring hearts and for all the guidance and support you gave me; not to mention all the help you gave me by caring for Navah and Kaya.

Maki, Toshi, and *Namika,* thank you for being in our lives. *Maki,* I value our friendship and partnership. I appreciate you taking the time to plan and coordinate as well as translate during our stay in the breathtaking town of Kamikatsu.

Zero Waste Program team of Kamikatsu, you rock! Thank you for all you do in making sure that Kamikatsu stays a zero-waste town. You're one of the most loving, caring, and hospitable people I have met. You're also a reminder of what life is all about.

To the staff of *Northcentral Bronx Hospital.* Thank you for treating Ed as a part of your family and the kindness and compassion you showed to him while he was battling cancer.

Serena and Carol, thank you for your friendship and love to both Ed and me. Serena, he called you "his best friend" and truly loved and cared for you and your daughters.

A big shout out to the *Jazz community,* especially to Bob DeVos and Carol Selman, JC Stylles, Akiko Tsuruga, Adrienne McKay, Pat Martino, Lou Donaldson, Dr. Lonnie Smith, Jack, Randi, and the Legion Post in Harlem-an amazing place to connect with the soul and listen to so many wonderful musicians and loving people.

Healing Hearts Bereavement Retreat, CancerCare, and *its kind donors,* for all the compassion and for all the wonderful services that you provide to so many families in times of sorrow. I experienced firsthand the love you share. Thank you for providing our family with the perfect space to grieve, remember, and celebrate our departed loved ones in such a magical and spiritual way. A special thank you to Kathy, Claire, Cecilia, and Ariana for all that you did for our family and countless other families. Thank you to the volunteers who make Healing Hearts happen in a very special way. A special thank you to Eisai for its financial contribution to making Healing Hearts a reality and its incredible employees who share their time and talents in supporting this worthy cause.

Thank you to *Mike and Norina Pasciuto.* I am inspired by your beautiful story and the love that led to your "two families becoming one." The DeAnna Pasciuto Foundation does incredible things for people impacted by cancer and helped to make Healing Hearts a reality for families like ours.

For bonus material go to ...

Alison Hoffman, I can't thank you enough for being such an amazing human being. Not only did you help Ed so much with all the needed resources during his stay at the hospital, but after his passing, you continued to show how much you cared by providing me with resources, such as CancerCare. Ed said to me once, "Jay, I love my social worker. She is the best!" You are the best! And Columbia Presbyterian Hospital is so lucky to have you in the bone marrow unit. My life has been transformed because of you. Thank you for sharing the old Yiddish word "bashert" with me. It truly feels like our families were meant to find each other!

Columbia Presbyterian Hospital, especially the bone marrow unit, *Dr. Jerci*, and all the hard-working and caring nurses and staff who went the extra mile to care for and bring comfort to so many patients and families like ours. God's love and compassion shine bright through you all. Thank you for being the magic in so many lives.

YM & YWHA Be Me after-school program staff, especially *Victoria* and *Katherine*, whose love, help, and kindness went beyond expectations. There is such much love here, not only for the children but for the families as well. Victoria, thank you again for the Russian art therapy class. My heart was filled with gratitude as I saw my girls create art with all the resources provided. The music and singing were enchanting, and just being there and listening transported me to another dimension. Seeing the girls talk about their loss with other children and with you was really empowering. I enjoyed the delicious treats we created during the class as a family.

Coach Lucrecia Noriega, you are one of a kind! I love you and thank you for the wonderful work you do to help others be the best that they can be and understand that they are bigger than their circumstances. I am grateful for your guidance and encouragement to write, write, and write until my book was done. I really enjoyed our sessions, the laughs, and the sharing of ideas.

Coach Yolanda Rodriguez Mayorga at the Centro Holistico de Transformacion Integral, I am sending you a hug filled with love. Thank you for guiding the path of so many in search of the light. I admire your big and gentle heart. I enjoyed our womb blessing therapy sessions as they helped me reconnect with my divine femine essence and healing the pain of losing Kai. I enjoyed our deep conversations and healing meditations.

Lupita Miguel, Spiritual Mentor, I am sending you a super hug filled with love and gratitude all the way to Morocco. *I want to take this opportunity to thank you for embracing my soul in such a loving, and compassionate way. I continue to hear you saying to me, "Nancy when in doubt ask yourself, "Am I acting from a place of fear or love? Then, let the answer guide your interactions and path in life. Remember that love transforms everything into harmony and happiness." I love you!*

Charo Zamarron, and *Norma Uribe,* at Espiritu Crystal Centro Holistico, it's with gratitude and admiration that I thank you for helping me heal my inner child, and for helping me grow spiritually as well as for guiding my path. Thank you for the amazing work you do. Sending you both a bear hug!

For bonus material go to ...

Northvale Public School, thank you so much for welcoming us with so much love to the community and for providing a safe and caring fresh start for our family.

I am so grateful to you, *Ryan Kirch,* for taking time out of your busy schedule to listen and look over my work. Somehow you still manage to give a helping hand to those who need you. And it's the same with your beautiful wife, Sarah. I can't thank her enough for all the planning and coordination she does to make sure that our children have well-rounded experiences outside school.

To *Carmen, Perla, Francia, Cristina, Ada, Clara, Alicia, Berenice, Charo,* and *Feliz Joel* at Sunscape Resort, Puerto Plata. I thank you with my heart filled with gratitude and admiration for all your love and for uplifting my soul as we gathered and shared Ed's memories from deep in our hearts.

Rossi and *Joan,* and the hard-working dedicated staff at *Refried Beans, Mexican Grill,* we thank you for being our escape place each and every time we returned to NYC from our vacations or outings. No matter what, we ended up at Refried Beans. I remember that after a few weeks of giving birth to Kaya, it was the first restaurant we visited. Kaya was a month old. There is so much love here and so many wonderful memories. Shortly after meeting Mike, Refried Beans was one of the places that we visited together with our girls to celebrate Ed. Rossi, regardless of the distance, your place will always have a special place in my heart. Keeva loves Refried Beans!

A big thank you to the *Mambi Restaurant and staff* for all the beautiful memories. This was the only place Ed and I would find herring with eggs and onion, the Dominican way. It was here that I met many friends, and where Mike and I had our first date! Thank you for making delicious herring.

Le Cheile, thank you for providing Ed and me and the girls with a lovely place, where Ed enjoyed one of his favorite dishes, fish and chips and Guinness. I remember that Ed and I visited Le Cheile during one of the visits home from the hospital. He had Irish tea with hot milk, and I had a cafe late. The girls love the mac and cheese!

181 Cabrini, thank you for providing an intimate place for Mike and I to get to know one another and bond over our experiences.

Pick and Eat is another memorable place for me, for many reasons. Not only did Ed and I love the healthy bites, green juices, and smoothies here, but it was also in this beautiful space that I posted my first photo exhibition in 2015. Mike and I had our second date here, and it was in the private and intimate space at Pick and Eat that he proposed. Alex, I will always be grateful to you and your staff for being so wonderful, and for your contribution to the community.

Thank you to *Guadalupe Restaurant,* which was to perfect place to enjoy delicious food and celebrate our engagement with our good friends Mark and Elba.

Thank you, *Saggios Restaurant,* for all the good times Ed and I shared. I love Italian food, and this is one of my favorite restaurants in Washington Heights. During our date nights, Ed

For bonus material go to ...

and I would eat here often. If we did not eat dinner here, we found ourselves there enjoying a drink and one of their delicious desserts. I remember meeting Francia at this special place after Ed and Alex's passing. It felt good to go back and be in this beautiful space with so many heartfelt memories.

Floridita Restaurant, thank you for the delicious "Café Cubano." Elba and I met here and enjoyed a delicious breakfast after losing Ed. We spent the time talking about him, and it felt good to share this with my good friend. It was a place where we both shared mutual feelings and the unexpected things that life brings.

Inwood Bar & Grill, thank you for being a warm and lively place to gather and celebrate life. Warm staff and delicious food. I remember celebrating Kaya's pre-K graduation here and meeting Ed after work for dinner many times. After Ed's passing, Serena and I met here and had a heart felt conversation about Ed, and the mutual love we both have for his beautiful soul.

A big shout out to *Mr. Brady's Fox Inn Restaurant* and the amazing staff. Thank you for welcoming us in such a beautiful and caring way. I remember that you called your daughter who worked in NYC, to come and talk to us about her commute when we were looking for a house here. Mike and I valued our conversations and laughs. We are grateful that you have opened your doors for us to gather year after year and celebrate Maria and Ed with families and friends.

YOU, the reader, thank you for supporting my journey by reading, sharing, and hopefully learning something from this book. You are beautiful and powerful and make this world a better place.

With a grateful heart, I thank the following organizations for contributing to the person I've become: John Bowne High School, *SUNY New Paltz, Lehman College of New York, City College, Touro University, Columbia University Head Start Program, Adelphi University Administrators forum* and *training programs, New York City Department of Education, Breathe for Change, the New York Public Library,* the *Cool Culture organization and* the *International Center of Photography (ICP).*

From the bottom of my heart, a big thank you to *Raymond, Andreah, Liz,* and the 10-10-10 Publishing Program for their guidance, support, and mentoring during my journey of writing this book.

Riverdale Funeral Home, Inc. Thank you to the staff for being so kind and gentle. This is a place where I found comfort and guidance not once, but twice.

Thank you, thank you, thank you to all the *Teachers* who are constantly in and out of my life and guiding my path both physically and spiritually.

Thank you to *God, life,* and our expanding *Universe* for allowing me to reconnect and see beyond what I thought I could see, and for the immense love and compassion I feel deep inside my heart.

About the Author

Nancy "Jay" is an educator, artist, and author who was born and raised in the Dominican Republic. She is a dedicated New York City public school teacher who earned a Big Apple Teacher's Award Recognition. Nancy holds multiple advanced degrees in various specializations. Her goal is to continue to write, speak, and coach to uplift and bring joy to others, as well as to illustrate that we are all special and worthy of a happy, abundant, and fulfilled life.

Nancy resides in New Jersey with her husband Mike, four daughters, their chihuahua Panchito, and their two betta fish, Blue Bell and Freddy.

She enjoys taking photos of nature and everyday moments as a reminder to be grateful for all that we have and all the beauty that surrounds us. Her last photo exhibition, "Joy in a Bubble," shares the innocence and simplicity of young souls connecting to the play dance of childhood. It was presented at the Hispanic Heritage Show at the Long Branch Arts and Cultural Center in Long Branch, New Jersey.

Nancy has over 20 years of experience working with children and families. Prior to working for the NYDOE, she was an administrator and educational supervisor for Columbia University Head Start in NYC.

For bonus material go to www.griefandgratitudebook.com

She received her Post Master's Degree in School Building and Leadership from City College of New York, her first Master's in Early Childhood, Special and Bilingual Education from Touro University, her Bachelor of Arts in Psychology from the State University of New York at New Paltz and a second Bachelor's Degree in Speech-Language/Audiology from Lehman College.

She completed her Breathe for Change Social-Emotional Learning Facilitator and yoga teacher certification. Her focus is to use mindfulness, yoga, and social-emotional learning as vehicles for healing and social change.

Nancy continues to coach and guide young people, particularly Latina immigrants like herself, in pursuing their educational goals and showing them that there are no limits to what they can achieve.

Connect with the Author

The author is available for delivering keynote presentations, workshops and retreats, as well as coaching and mentoring.

Her services are available in English and/or Spanish.

For rates and availability, please contact Nancy directly at: GriefandGratitudebook.com.

You can also go to her website to order more books and free downloads.

Finally, if you have been inspired by this book, the best thing you can do is pass it on as a way to radiate your love and gratitude and to support others in their own healing and life journey. We are all linked and when we uplift others, we are uplifting ourselves.

- nancyjalowiecki
- @nancyjalowiecki
- @nancyjalowiecki

Made in the USA
Middletown, DE
09 February 2023